JUSTICE MATTERS

Rescuing the
legal system for
the twenty-first century

Roberta R. Katz
with
Philip Gold

Published by the Discovery Institute
Seattle, Washington, USA
Copyright 1997 by
Roberta R. Katz
and Philip Gold

Justice Matters: Rescuing the legal system for the twenty-first century

Roberta R. Katz and Philip Gold.

ISBN   0-9638654-1-2

Limited first edition published by Discovery Institute 1997

Discovery Institute
Seattle, Washington, USA
www.discovery.org

*The judicial power of the United States,
shall be vested in one supreme Court, and in
such inferior Courts as the Congress may
from time to time ordain and establish.*

*The Constitution of the United States
Article III
Section 1*

JUSTICE MATTERS

Preface by Philip Gold

The law can be no single thing. It never has been. Throughout history, law has been perceived as everything from the will of God to the means by which some groups oppress others. Today, ask a hundred off-the-shelf Americans (assuming such creatures still exist) to define the civil justice system — that part of the legal system dealing with non-criminal but culpable conduct and dispute resolution — and many would probably echo the laconic Sgt. Friday of that old TV series, *Dragnet*: "The rules, ma'am. Just the rules." And most, no doubt, would add immediately thereafter something along the lines of: "Protecting my rights."

Rules and rights. Rights and rules. Entirely true, but far from the entire truth. Aristotle once defined man biologically as a "featherless biped" and socially as a "political animal," literally, a being who lives in a *polis*. But "featherless biped" can also describe a plucked chicken, and the crabbed "rights and rules" definition seems appropriate to what so many of us feel we've become: plucked chickens living in large cities. But there's far more to it than that, and *Justice Matters* shows the way.

I got involved with this project absent-mindedly. Like many Discovery Institute fellows, I have more than one specialty. I do defense and national security work, but also hold a doctorate in modern U.S. cultural history, which I've written about and taught for twenty years. My legal background's nil, but Roberta needed someone to book-doctor an early draft, and I thought it might prove an interesting diversion. Sure, why not?

My historian's instinct soon told me that it was much more.

Justice Matters combines an astute assessment of a clear and present danger with a plan for action *now*. And it goes beyond the legal and the technical to offer several important insights into where this country is headed, and why.

In essence, Roberta makes three vital points. First, the current civil justice system is neither an unchanging absolute nor a modern quirk. It developed over a millennium to correct procedures gone archaic and dysfunctional, to meet new needs, and to advance fundamental principles of fairness, equity, and justice. The system's in bad trouble now. Its problems are structural. And it's time for the next restructuring, if the system's fundamental principles are to be preserved and strengthened... and if Americans are to find in their courts, once again, the quality of justice they expect and require.

Second, Roberta shows that the Information Age now upon us requires both entirely new and "back to the future" approaches if the civil justice system is to evolve to handle 21st century problems, and if the system itself is to be brought into the Information Age. Historically, there's nothing unusual about this. Every successful renaissance, every effective reformation combines these approaches. Only the failures concentrate on the future or the past exclusively. It's never either/or.

Finally, Roberta raises the issue of civil law's place in a diverse, fragmented, Information Age society. Law never can be entirely instrumental. It codifies some of our deepest beliefs about how human beings should relate to and deal with each other, indeed, our deepest beliefs about what human life ought to be. But can law do this – should it even try – in an era such as ours?

The answer is, I believe, today more than ever. It's commonplace to say that ours is a transitional era. Of course. All eras are. But this era may also, I believe, be described as an "inter-canonical" era – a time between two canons, two sets of commonly held beliefs about who and what we are, what we should be doing, and how we should be doing it. Law is always a vital part of any set of shared beliefs, along with literature, art, history, science, philosophy, and faith.

Roberta suggests that many of the problems with the current justice system reflect, and are intensified by, the breakdown of the larger commonalities. Quite so. Many of the problems that plague the law cannot be solved by the law. But to the extent that her proposals are adopted, or even seriously discussed, law will become part of the larger struggle to achieve a new, more perfect canon: a struggle that I believe is already underway, although not yet clearly visible. And that new set of shared beliefs, when it rises out of the current welter of diversity, animosity, technological revolution, and cultural goo, will surely be as astonishing (and hopefully as glorious) as the medieval canon that arose out of those three utterly disparate heritages: the Judeo-Christian, the Greco-Roman, and the barbarian.

And that is why *Justice Matters* is a vital book in two ways. It is, first and foremost, a dead-on critique of the present system and a provocative, logical set of reform proposals. But it is also an impassioned groping toward a new civil justice system that should, that will, take its place in the 21st century canon-under-construction. America needs to know about it, as both legal issue and as paradigm for other struggles in other fields. *Justice Matters* is a profoundly moral as well as practical book.

And that, too, can serve as paradigm.

A Note To Readers by Roberta R. Katz

If it ain't broke, don't fix it.
A wise bit of advice, usually. But when something as important as America's civil justice system is clearly headed for breakdown – indeed, when breakdown may be imminent – then, at the very least, it's time to start thinking seriously about what's wrong and what fixing that system might entail.

That's why I've written *Justice Matters*.

Before presenting my analysis and recommendations, five points may require clarification. First, this book is intended for two distinct yet complementary audiences. I have written it for my fellow lawyers, many of whom already sense real danger in this crisis, and who are key to moving serious legal reform from proposal to reality. Lawyers who read this book (and I include here those lawyers who now serve as judges, legal educators, and legislators) may come to feel that I have oversimplified the complexities and nuances of the civil justice system. They may also feel that I focus excessively on the system from the perspective of non-lawyers. I ask their forbearance, and offer as justification the fact that this book is also intended for lay people who have an enduring and compelling interest in the system as taxpayers, jurors, and litigants. And I ask the forbearance of lay readers, should they from time to time encounter too much Legalese. Terms such as "discovery" and *"stare decisis"* I've included only when necessary, and have provided plain English definitions for non-lawyers.

In short, I have written for attorneys and clients (and poten-

9

tial clients), and for these groups in their roles as citizens. I hope that each audience will appreciate the difficulty of writing for two groups. And I hope they will also appreciate the benefits. If we can achieve at least a minimal commonality, then dialogue between lawyers and non-lawyers can be more constructive.

Second, there are two groups that I haven't written for. One is the community of academic legal experts. This book is a practical analysis of a serious problem and a set of recommendations for reform. It is not an exhaustive scholarly tome. The experts will find much to argue with here, and I expect to learn much from their comments. But my purpose is to work toward real-world change, and that purpose remains primary. Also, I haven't written this book for those who have already made up their minds that there is not and will not be any crisis. They doubtless have their reasons, ranging from economic self-interest to ideological rigidity. I neither attempt nor expect to persuade them. Still, I do hope to persuade those whose resistance comes from an understandable and all-too-human reluctance to embrace new ways of doing things, especially after the old ways have been so laboriously learned and perfected.

Third, this book deals with America's civil justice system. However, it includes various references to the criminal justice system. Obviously, the two share a number of characteristics, especially in their reliance on adversarial proceedings: prosecution versus defendant in the criminal context, plaintiff versus defendant in the civil. However, because the criminal justice system contains unique rules and constitutional protections, and because it has its own crises and travails, I do not deal with it. If any of my recommendations for reform have relevance to the criminal system, that's an additional benefit. But in this context, they apply to the civil system only.

Fourth, one cannot say everything at once. Throughout this

book, I raise questions concerning legal ethics, relate these matters to changes in the larger society, and in turn tie these to the challenges and opportunities of the Information Age. I plan to return to these matters in future articles and in my next book. For now, real-world crisis and practical reform are my main concerns.

Finally, the matter of voice. Although this book is a shared effort, passages using "I" refer to me alone. When the first person plural appears in the text, it refers to all of us – "we" as in "we Americans."

That said, it is a pleasant duty to give credit to the many people who have played significant parts in the writing of this book. Though I cannot begin to name them all, I certainly do thank them all. The thinking and writing in these pages are the product of my own passion for the subject and concern about our future. But they also reflect the views of many others, inside and outside the legal profession, who seek to understand the problems and restore the system.

Still, there are a few individuals who have played vital roles in the development of this book. First and foremost is my husband of 28 years. Chuck Katz is the kind of lawyer all lawyers aspire to be. He is a highly valued counselor, a man of keen intelligence and impeccable morality, and someone clients trust absolutely with their most precious ideas and assets. For many years now, he has been an unfailingly patient and responsive sounding board for my ideas, a generous contributor to my efforts, and an extraordinarily supportive partner. He was always there with an encouraging word when I needed it. Thank you.

This book might have been written, but would have been far less readable, in every sense of the word, had I not had the good fortune to meet and then work with Philip Gold, my colleague

11

at Discovery Institute and my co-author. After the first draft was completed, Philip agreed, out of the goodness of his heart, to help with the revision of the text. That help grew into much more. He gave my words an expressiveness they hadn't had before, and he enhanced – in ways that were at times subtle and at times dramatic – the quality of thought reflected in the book. I had to twist his arm, though, to get him to put his name on the cover. He demurred at first because he's not an attorney and felt that his inclusion might affect the book's credibility in legal circles. But I'm proud to say that this is very much a collaborative effort. Thank you.

I also thank Bruce Chapman, founder and president of Discovery Institute, who talked me into the project in the first place. Then he kept after me, challenging my ideas and, in some magical way that I still don't understand, constantly moving me to higher and better planes of thought. I shudder to think what this book would have looked like, Bruce, had we stopped when I thought it was done.

Others helped me to "not stop." A generous grant from the SAFECO Corporation accelerated the effort. Discovery's Board of Directors provided several excellent early critics, especially Eileen Odum of GTE and Ray Waldmann of Boeing. Attorney Anthony Lowe and Seattle University law student/Discovery Institute intern David Pringle did vital research and offered valuable suggestions. Rob Crowther, Discovery's director of public and media relations, presided over the physical production and publicity (and performed his usual miracles with the Institute's computers). Claudia Vernia of Vernia Design, Seattle, did the cover.

Three others, friends and colleagues of many years, helped me refine my thinking through discussions about civil justice reform over many years. Each of them, in his or her own way, has made a mark on the book. Thank you, Tom Alberg, John Jester, and Maura O'Neill.

Then there is Jim Barksdale, for several years now my boss and also my mentor, who has graciously indulged my after-hours writing and who made it possible for me to be at Netscape. There I've been privileged to get an early glimpse of what the future is going to be. Thank you, Jim.

Finally, I wish to thank my two daughters, Sarah and Sydney, both very talented and special people in their own right. They knew my thoughts might be controversial, and one of them even advised me to write under a pseudonym. But again and again they have been there for me with their love, their young but profound wisdom, and their support. I hope I have done them justice.

Introduction

We Americans hold dear our system of laws. We should, for the legal system is the very foundation of our common life. Our governments enact, administer, interpret, and enforce laws. Our citizens encounter law, and the effects of law, in virtually every daily activity – driving, working, finding a home, raising children, playing sports, shopping, paying taxes, and the myriad other aspects of living and dying. The legal system pervades our lives more thoroughly than does any other civil institution.

So when the system – in this case, the civil justice system by which we resolve our non-criminal disputes – settles into a condition of chronic crisis and seems headed toward outright collapse, it's time to face the fact and start finding solutions. For failure to act entails more than accepting a dysfunctional and unjust system that imposes enormous and unnecessary costs on the American economy and society. Ultimately, it also contributes to the erosion of the moral fiber of the citizenry.

We Americans also cherish our belief that the law protects the rights and responds to the needs of all citizens. Ours is a system "of the people, by the people, and for the people." Accordingly, we hold dear the right of every citizen to go to court and to use the system to seek remedies for grievance. This right is as vital to the maintenance of our society as are the state's own law enforcement activities. And indeed, it is a right that more and more people are now asserting. Whether this go-to-court trend bodes well or ill for society is debatable, but clearly it is perilous for a litigious people to have to depend upon an increasingly erratic and inequitable civil justice system.

Most plaintiffs don't think of themselves as going to court for lofty societal purposes. They go to "get even" or "make someone pay," as a result of a dispute or grievance. But when a dispute or grievance goes to court, its nature changes. It is no longer simply a matter between two disputants, but becomes a matter in which society – represented by a judge and a jury – claims an interest. The judge and the jury are expected to resolve the dispute, based upon an impartial determination of who and what is right under the law. This is why the judge "instructs" the jury on what principles of law it must apply to the facts of the case. This is also why "jury nullification" —in which a jury affirmatively ignores the law in making its decision— can threaten the stability and predictability of justice.

By and large, over the past two centuries, the American civil justice system has worked well. Most people have respected the courts and their role, even if this high regard did not always extend to the lawyers who guided the litigants through the process. But over the last few years, this has changed. There is a growing sense that the court system is not working properly, and therefore a growing distrust of law. Some high-visibility cases, televised and the subject of continuous media commentary, have shown Americans the inner workings of the court system. Many are distressed by what they see. Disturbing civil cases and decisions now routinely make the news, such as a jury's large monetary award (later reduced during appeal) to a woman who claimed that McDonald's *broke the law* by selling her coffee that was too hot. Even more depressingly routine are stories about cases that drag on for years and ruin defendants: of obstetricians who have given up delivering babies for fear of lawsuits (or who can't afford malpractice insurance); of people getting rich because somebody else made an insulting comment or told a stupid joke.

Anecdotal evidence may be just that: anecdotal. But the stories cumulate, and few people seem surprised anymore when they learn of preposterous lawsuits . . . or preposterous verdicts and awards.

As citizens, concerned about the integrity of the system, we know that something is wrong. We're worried. We ought to be. In fact, we should be appalled by the growing popular opinion that justice is no longer being served in the courts, and by the volume of cases that justify that negative opinion. Just one small example. A 1995 survey conducted by Public Opinion Strategies for the American Tort Reform Association revealed that between 60 and 80 percent of the American people have strong misgivings about the civil justice system's internal workings and decision-making. Significantly, those who had personal experience with the system, especially jury service, had less confidence than those who had none.[1]

Such deep doubts indicate a clear and present danger. Loss of respect for what happens in the court system ultimately means loss of respect for the law, and loss of respect for the law can be fatal to a democracy – especially a diverse democracy now deeply into a prolonged period of rapid change and chronic stress. For without law, there is no encoded social bond or limit to the exercise of public and private power. Without such a bond, without such limitations, the way is opened to anarchy or tyranny. When criminal or civil justice falters, people either take matters into their own hands or cede them to some strong governmental force. And a vicious spiral is set in motion. Anarchy justifies tyranny. Tyranny begets anarchy.

Neither is acceptable. And that is why the legal system must be set aright.

I'm a lawyer. Over the past fifteen years, I have been a partner in one of the country's largest law firms and have served as general counsel of three publicly-held high-tech companies. I also hold a doctorate in cultural anthropology, with specialization in the study of social change. As a lawyer, I'm concerned for my profession. As an anthropologist, I can sense how the crisis of the civil justice system relates to this society's other problems. As a citizen, I'm worried for the country. And as a mother, I fear for my children's future, for the futures of all our kids who, if present trends continue, will live with, and suffer under, a civil justice system reduced to an ugly mix of lottery, gladiatorial combat, and farce.

This book has three sections. Part One, "Civil Justice: Where It Came from, Where It Went," begins with two preliminary sketches: of the system's basic structure and processes, and of the major popular (and also professional) criticisms of that system's current workings. I then suggest that these criticisms, though valid, miss the major point. To wit: The present civil justice system, far from existing as some ahistorical absolute, is a product of the needs of the Industrial Era, and unsuited to the 21st century. In fact, many of the present abuses are possible only because of the growing obsolescence of the system. Greed and viciousness we always have with us. But we are also living with a system that, because of its intensifying dysfunctions, *actually rewards such qualities*. This must change.

In Part Two, "Civil Justice for the New Millennium," I argue that the civil justice system, like every other institution, must adapt its workings to the forces which have converged upon us: computerization, globalization, ever-increasing complexity, and accelerating change. I note again – a matter of vital importance here – that the present civil justice system, the adversary system, did not emerge full-blown and perfect at some definite point in the past. Rather, it evolved over a thousand years. In its present form, the adversary system is a confluence of elements, each of which developed to address needs and abuses of the past. This is vital:

> *While the adversary system enshrines and reifies certain basic principles which must be kept, none of the system's components, in their present form, is immutable. In fact, serious change is necessary in order to preserve the principles and virtues of the system. So it has been throughout legal history. So it is today.*

After developing this point, I look at the present array of proposals and experiments . . . and at some of the cries of frustration emanating from bench and bar that point toward further change. Then I present my own plan for addressing present problems and adapting the civil justice system to the needs of the 21st century. Included in my plan is a proposal to organize new courts, and a new court system, by the kinds of subjects they must consider. I call these CORE Courts, an acronym standing for "COmmonality/REsolution." The idea is to form courts around commonalities or communities of activity and interest, with emphasis on dispute resolution and problem-solving through procedures adapted to each court's different subject-matter.

In Part Three, "Toward Justice in Cyberspace," I offer some reflections and predictions on how new computer and communications technologies may ultimately transform the very nature of litigation: everything from procedural revolutions to "virtual" legal actions in which the contending parties may never enter a physical court house.

At this point, two caveats are in order. First, none of the individual proposals I offer here is entirely original. Procedural and evidentiary reforms have been studied to death over the past two decades. Some promising experiments are underway. There also has been a growing popular literature, some of it sensationalistic, some thoughtful. But, to the best of my knowledge, this is the first time these ideas have been assembled and presented as a comprehensive package, intended to meet the needs of the 21st century as well as to correct present abuses. In this sense, I believe I have gone beyond these prior efforts. And I hope that this package will prove to be more than the sum of its parts.

Second, I am fully aware of how difficult it would be to implement these proposals. CORE Courts can be arranged in many different ways: by technical area, by industry, by activity, and by physical community for some issues. Personnel and certification issues could be complex and volatile. The problem of preserving and enforcing constitutional guarantees is present throughout. Implementation would necessarily take many years. Inevitably, some experiments may fail, or demonstrate the need for even more fundamental change. But these difficulties are not show-stoppers. Understanding and then dealing with them, while time-consuming and challenging, are essential tasks in building an effective legal system for the future.

Finally, let me acknowledge that many people will resist the premise of this book. They will argue that the present system is basically sound, that it operates as its founders and previous generations of custodians intended. I also know that many lawyers and judges will, consciously or subconsciously, perceive my views as harmful to their own outlooks and interests. After delivering many speeches on this topic to groups of lawyers, I know how distressed they sometimes get. As one lawyer confided to me after a speech to a state bar association: "You made me want to run out of the room. My gut was telling me to be angry with you, but my head told me that I needed to stay because what you said was making sense."

I have no wish to harm my fellow lawyers. And, although this book often focuses on the dilemmas of defendants, I have no wish to limit the legitimate rights and abilities of aggrieved plaintiffs and their counsel. To the contrary, my purpose here is to redeem the system for both sides: to take an adversarial system run amok and, by rendering it more relevant and less adversarial, by making it *more true to its own origins and spirit*, to strengthen the values that system was established to uphold. These are nothing less than the principles of rational and dependable justice and dispute resolution, competently administered and properly dispensed.

I'm not a critic-for-criticism's sake, or unmindful that I've enjoyed a fulfilling career as an attorney. But I am persuaded that if the legal profession ignores the problem or, even worse, pretends that nothing is amiss, ultimately both the profession and the people will suffer.

And I hope just as fervently that, in the end, the angels of our better nature will prevail. They must prevail. For the more diverse and complex this society becomes, the greater is the need for a legal system that makes it possible for us to live together in fairness, decency, and dignity. And perhaps it is not too much to suggest that the very task of crafting such a system could teach us a few useful lessons in how to get along outside the courtroom as well as in it.

1 American Tort Reform Association, *"Executive Summary: National Survey on Legal Liability Reform Issue,"* done by Public Opinion Strategies, Alexandria, Va. 1995.

I. CIVIL JUSTICE: WHERE IT CAME FROM, WHERE IT WENT

CHAPTER ONE
THE SYSTEM AND ITS
DISCONTENTS

Everybody knows what happens at a trial. Two impassioned lawyers hurl brilliant barbs at and past each other, demolish hostile witnesses by deftly raising an eyebrow or two, shout *"Objection, Your Honor!"* at least once every five minutes, and generally pace about the courtroom, dazzling the assemblage by their logic, wit, and command of detail. Finally, one of them wins the case with a summation that leaves the jury in an advanced state of exhaustion, exaltation, and rapture, and the opposing attorney already beginning to cherish the honor of having been beaten by this demigod of the bar. We've seen it all before, in the movies and on TV.

Of course, it doesn't work that way. Courtrooms can be places of high drama, but more often they're places where procedures methodically play themselves out – procedures whereby two opposing parties argue their cases before a neutral presiding judge and a neutral, passive jury of "peers." The scene seems so natural that it's hard to realize just how recent a phenomenon it is, or to keep in mind that other ways may render justice equally well, or even better.

Before discussing the origins and breakdown of the system, it will be useful, especially for non-lawyers, to do two things: sketch the basic workings of the civil justice system, then reprise the "standard" list of complaints about that system. Then we'll look at why the civil justice system – that remarkable "joint venture" of adversarial parties and their counsel, neutral and passive decision-makers on the bench and in the jury box, and precise rules of procedure and evidence – is breaking down, and why neither partial fixes (no matter how useful) nor the legal profession's penchant for "non-binding self-flagellation" are sufficient responses. One conclusion will begin to emerge:

Today, the logic of the system itself, and the ideals underlying that logic, mandate far-reaching change.

The Substance of the Contest: Facts and Law

The American civil justice system is primarily an adversarial system, pitting a plaintiff against a defendant and letting them and their counsels present their best evidence and arguments in accordance with required procedures and standards. In theory, and generally in practice, the system is passive, although this has been changing a bit in recent years. Unlike an inquisitorial system, which actively seeks out cases and evidence, the civil adversary system waits for someone to bring a complaint, then requires the other party to respond. In most cases, by the time a trial opens, an enormous amount of work has already been done. The courtroom provides the climactic confrontation and leads to the decision-making functions of the jury and the judge.

The present adversary system assigns different yet equally important substantive roles to the judge and the jury. In general, the jury is required to decide the facts of the case. The judge determines which laws are relevant to the case. But "facts" and "law" are not always obvious.

The Facts (And the Rules that Help Determine Them)

Facts are sometimes hard to discern. Two people watching the same event can derive very different impressions. People sometimes deliberately distort facts for their own purposes, or hide them, or deny their existence. But in a lawsuit, the facts must be established before determining whether any violation of law has occurred.

For example, in a tort case where the plaintiff claims that the defendant wrongfully harmed him or her, the first requirement is to settle the factual questions about the nature, source, and extent of the plaintiff's injuries (if any). Only then is it possible to pursue the question of whether the defendant's actions or inactions were "negligent," "grossly negligent," or "intentional." Similarly, in a contract dispute, it is vital to determine just what the contract says and what the parties involved did or did not do. Only then is it possible to decide whether a "breach of contract" has occurred.

At the trial level, most of the courtroom fight is about the facts. Typically, the plaintiff's lawyers and supporting witnesses try to convince the jury of their version, while the defendant's lawyers and witnesses offer their own scenario. In order to tell their stories, however, each side must follow certain well-defined rules.

In a civil case, the Rules of Civil Procedure and the Rules of Evidence apply. The Federal Rules of Civil Procedure, which are promulgated under the authority of the U.S. Supreme Court and approved by Congress, apply to lawsuits filed in federal courts. State court systems have their own rules of procedure. These generally parallel the federal rules. However, state rules may differ from federal rules, and from state to state. Regardless of the source, the Rules of Civil Procedure define the general structure of the contest. They dictate, for example:

- The forms of the documents needed to start and continue a lawsuit.
- The means by which a defendant must be notified of the lawsuit in order for the parties officially to be engaged.
- The time limits for various moves and countermoves and the penalties that result from failure to meet deadlines.
- Rules relating to jury selection.
- Special kinds of judgments and lesser decisions known as "motions," because they are made in response to a move, or motion, by one of the parties in the case.
- When and how one party can obtain, or "discover," information from the other party for use in the case.

During the pre-trial period, the months or years between the date the plaintiff files the lawsuit and the start of the courtroom trial, rules regarding discovery are the most important. These govern how the parties develop the facts by use of different tools and techniques, including interrogatories (written requests for answers), depositions (sworn statements), and the production of "documents and things." Each of these areas has its own set of sub-rules.

The rules governing discovery mandate an extremely broad right to seek information – a right established in its present form only a half century ago. As Federal Rule of Procedure 26(b)(1) states: In general, "[p]arties may obtain discovery regarding any matter, not privileged, which is relevant to the subject matter involved in the pending action, whether it relates to the claim or defense of the party seeking discovery or to the claim or defense of any other party, including the existence, description, nature, custody, condition, and location of any books, documents, or other tangible things and the identity and location of persons having knowledge of any discoverable matter. The information sought need not be admissible at the trial if the information sought appears reasonably calculated to lead to the discovery of admissible evidence."

Once the trial starts, the Rules of Evidence govern the development of fact. As with the Rules of Civil Procedure, there are separate but usually parallel rules of evidence in place for federal and state trial courts. In essence, these intricate rules create categories of information and then prescribe which categories may be offered to the jury through the testimony of witnesses and the presentation of exhibits. A lawyer's skill in employing the Rules of Evidence can be vital. If a crucial piece of information cannot be presented to the jury, for trial purposes that information – even if true – does not exist. Therefore, a great deal of courtroom maneuvering relates to the Rules of Evidence.

Further, the Rules of Evidence do not necessarily reflect common-sense notions of what matters. For example, evidence of wrongdoing contained in lawyer-client correspondence may be excluded on the grounds that it is "privileged." There are various other kinds of privileges in our legal system, which also protect information from disclosure in order to support certain special relationships. Such other privileges include the priest-penitent privilege and the doctor-patient privilege. For similar reasons, information may be excluded because it was improperly or unconstitutionally obtained. Moreover, information provided by a third party not present to testify may be excluded as "hearsay," unless one of 24 specific exceptions to the hearsay exclusion applies.

In sum, before trial, the discovery portion of the Rules of Civil Procedure governs the processes by which the parties develop the facts of the case. During the trial, the Rules of Evidence determine what information may be presented to the jury (or judge, in a juryless trial), who determines the facts. The next step involves application of the law to the facts.

The Law

The judge applies the law to the facts by looking at two sources of law: statutes and "common" or "case" law.

Statutes are laws made by legislatures. As the term is used here, it also includes the Constitution (and its state counterparts), which sets forth our most fundamental rights and which therefore underlies and governs all other laws. Statutes generally speak for themselves, although not without interpretation and amplification. Courts interpret statutes, sometimes consulting a law's written legislative history or other evidence regarding the intent of the drafters. In this procedure, which applies to constitutional and statutory matters, judges first look at the literal words, then bring in other guidance as necessary. Such evidence becomes crucial when old laws, including the Constitution, are applied to circumstances that the authors did not foresee or could not have imagined.

Agencies also "make" law by writing procedures and regulations for the laws they must implement, and through the apparatus of administrative law. Many agencies, such as the Federal Trade Commission, have their own administrative court systems. The ability of statutory law to generate mountains of interpretation is legendary. A prime example: the tens of thousands of pages of tax regulations written by the U.S. Treasury Department.

Common or case law tends to be far less precise. American jurisprudence follows the English principle of *stare decisis,* under which courts are bound to follow the law established by earlier decisions, usually at the appellate level, in their jurisdiction. This means that, if the courts of a jurisdiction once determined that a defendant's actions were legally wrongful, when different parties later present the same or analogous sets of facts, the court is obliged to follow the law of the prior case. This chain of decision is known as "following legal precedent."

Within common law, there is considerable room for maneuver. Courtroom competition turns on the rival attorneys' persistence, logical skills, and oral and written powers of persuasion. Persistence may be required when a lawyer needs to find a prior case that decided the law favorably in relation to his or her client's case. Once such a precedent is located, the lawyer must convince the court that this prior case more closely resembles the present matter than do the prior cases being presented by the opposing lawyer.

Precedents can conflict for many reasons. Occasionally, judges and juries make mistakes. Sometimes they ignore precedent deliberately. More typically, the problem stems from the human ability to make intricate and subtle logical distinctions, i.e., to be convinced by an attorney that case X is really more relevant than case Y. Thus, similar cases can create different precedents.

After determining the facts of the case and the relevant laws and precedents, it is necessary to apply the law to the facts. The judge may order that some action be undertaken or stopped. The jury may award damages, concluding that the plaintiff did indeed suffer losses, material or nonmaterial ("pain and suffering"), translatable into a set amount of dollars. In some jurisdictions, the jury may award punitive damages, additional money to the plaintiff to punish a defendant deemed guilty of serious misbehavior. Compensatory and punitive damage awards can run from the pitifully inadequate to the preposterously huge. The judge may overrule the jury. Juries may deadlock. Cases may be appealed. Many outcomes are possible, given the same sets of facts and law. And therein lies part of the problem in this rapidly changing society.

GROWING CONCERNS ABOUT FAIRNESS

It is clear – it has always been clear – that the legal system does not function with mathematical precision. Because of differences in legal skills, because of the room for maneuver afforded by rules, and because of the inexact nature of precedent, opportunities for unfairness and injustice coexist with their opposites. But, increasingly, Americans feel that civil litigation is not being conducted fairly . . . and that this unfairness goes far beyond the "traditional" and occasional injustices. Over the past few years, many Americans – especially those who have extensive contact with the system – have begun to feel that unfairness is now *systemic*.

Not surprisingly, some of this concern is expressed in negative attitudes toward attorneys and their conduct. Attorneys are probably the most visible part of the system, and the most highly compensated. People who may be reluctant to condemn the system as a whole can "take it out" on the lawyers, in much the same way that dislike for certain presidents or legislators stops short of disrespect for the White House or Congress. Still, negative attitudes toward attorneys and their behavior have reached a point that indicates that something deeper must be involved. In 1986, for example, the American Bar Association's (ABA) Commission on Professionalism reported that only six percent of corporations surveyed called "all or most lawyers" deserving of the title "professional."[1] A 1993 *National Law Journal* poll found that almost a third of all Americans considered lawyers "less honest than most people."[2] Since then, in survey after survey, this trend has intensified.

Further – and at least as ominous – there is within the legal profession a growing uneasiness, a sense that the bar had better get its own house in order. Experts are coming to share the opinion of the laity. This convergence is happening for two different but related reasons. As William Ide, then-president of the ABA, wrote to the nation's lawyers in 1993:

"[N]ow is the time for us as individuals and as a profession to pause and reflect. We need to seriously examine the reasons that relate to the public dissatisfaction with the legal profession. . . . Columnist George Will recently pondered this issue in a *Newsweek* commentary. [He wrote] 'As traditional sources of social norms – families, schools, churches – weaken, law seeps into the vacuum.'

" Wherever we turn, whatever specialty we practice, we see the signs that the law is carrying too much of society's burden. Our justice system today is unable to meet the current demands and expectations of society, much less progress toward the ideals envisioned by the founders after the Revolutionary War. . . . Legal institutions created many years ago weren't designed to handle the complex issues and burdensome caseloads we routinely see in our courtrooms.

"What is needed today is nothing short of a revolution in our administration of justice. . . . Should the public confidence be lost in the government to be fair and equitable through our justice system, we will only be sowing and nurturing the seeds of a real revolution that no one wants. In reality, there is no choice, when you consider the alternatives."[3]

Mr. Ide (with a little help from Mr. Will) reveals the two reasons lawyers now experience a certain uneasiness . . . and why the public's "traditional" skepticism concerning lawyers has segued into something more serious. First, rightly or wrongly, society now expects the legal system to provide the kinds of social ordering and value-formation once left to the "mediating institutions" between the government and the individual. Why this has happened is beyond the scope of this book. It is sufficient to note here that increasing burdens for the legal system are a fact of life.

Mr. Ide's second point is also crucial. It is, in fact, the central conundrum of the civil justice system. Simply put, *as Americans have come to demand more of their legal system, they have also come to have less faith in its fairness.* And cosmetic or peripheral reforms cannot begin to restore either the system's fairness or the citizenry's faith.

Before discussing the deeper, systemic problems, it will be useful to consider the three particulars of the popular and, to some extent, the professional indictment of the legal system.

There Are Too Many Lawyers in the United States.

This continues to be the most prevalent theory, if only because it's the easiest to latch onto. Lawyers, so the argument goes, are not merely bad, at least by comparison with previous generations of attorneys. They are also multiplying at an alarming rate. Specifics of the complaint include: This new breed of lawyers is too greedy; lawyers are now businesspeople, not professionals; and lawyers have a lock on this ever-expanding legal system, which they manipulate for their own ends. And inevitably, flaws within the profession are exacerbated by larger social changes and by the increase in the profession's numbers and reach.

To take them in order:

It is difficult to determine what might be the "right" number of lawyers for this country. Comparisons with other countries don't reveal all that much, given that those performing legal work abroad are not always identified as lawyers. The United States, for example, currently has over 900,000 lawyers, or nearly 300 per hundred thousand population. Japan has about 11 per hundred thousand. Is either number "right"?

Cultural differences must be taken into account. Recently, a

Japanese bar association official, Koji Yanase, commented on why there were half as many lawyers in his country as in the Greater Washington, DC area. Said Mr. Yanase: "If an American is hit on the head by a ball at the ballpark, he sues. If a Japanese person is hit on the head he says, 'It's my honor. It's my fault. I shouldn't have been standing there.'"[4] Whatever the truth of the comparison, it doesn't seem entirely reasonable for a litigious people to complain about the ample supply of attorneys eager to handle their cases. Similarly, in contrast to other countries, our governmental structures create and sustain legal work: EPA, OSHA, IRS, ERISA, and ADA regulations, to name a few, each keep thousands of lawyers busy.

Another source of the "too many lawyers" sentiment may well derive from popular and sensationalized entertainments such as "LA Law" and the fictional output of John Grisham, among others. Most Americans have more contact with television and novels than with the civil justice system itself. This can lead to a curious misapprehension. Analysis of the "population" of the prime time television "universe" reveals a world comprised of about 30 percent cops, criminals, and lawyers: rather a dramatic overrepresentation. Further, entertainment, by its nature, emphasizes the dramatic, the melodramatic, and the extreme. A cockpit proverb describes aviation as "hours of boredom punctuated by seconds of terror." An equivalent adage might describe the practice of law as "weeks of routine punctuated by minutes of drama." But the weeks of boredom don't make it onto the screen.

An additional source of the "too many" sensibility may lie in the popular conception of law school as a default choice for bright college graduates who aren't sure what else to do, but know they like money and have to tell the parents *something*. Perhaps an old *New Yorker* cartoon captured this sentiment best when it showed a woman talking to a man at a cocktail party. The caption: "How did I know you're a lawyer? Easy. Everybody's a lawyer."

Finally, the behavior of some over-publicized, arrogance-is-my-trademark, take-no-prisoners attorneys contributes to this sense: a fact not lost on the profession, which now finds pleas for civility a regular feature of bar association literature.

A more fundamental complaint, and one that also resonates within the legal community, is that lawyers have become too aggressive, even entrepreneurial, in their pursuit of cash. Traditionally, lawyers could not (overtly) solicit business. A respectable professional waited until people came to him or her. To drum up business was "ambulance chasing." To do it too conspicuously was cause for professional censure. However, in 1977, in *Bates v. State Bar of Arizona,* the Supreme Court upheld the right of lawyers to advertise.[5] This opened the floodgates. Advertising led to more aggressive solicitation. The increasing use of contingent-fee arrangements – taking a percentage of the plaintiff's settlement in lieu of an hourly fee – encouraged the entrepreneurial ethos. The rise of class-action lawsuits, sometimes involving tens of thousands of people, propelled some lawyers toward extreme aggressiveness in seeking out large groups of "clients," only a few of whom would be actively involved in the case.

This is new. Fixed hourly fees have always provided at least a subliminal incentive to drag out the work. But when an attorney can make millions in contingent fees with just one victory, the incentive to sue, and to "take no prisoners," increases by orders of magnitude. Once a lawyer has a vested interest in the outcome of a suit, it becomes reasonable to encourage the client to seek the sun, moon, and stars . . . especially if juries are perceived as willing to grant astronomical awards.

The problem of greed, like the problems of aggressiveness and incivility, are acknowledged by the profession. Attempts are underway to formulate and enforce new and renewed standards of professional conduct. But greed and abrasiveness are hardly confined to the legal profession. Imagine what the system would be like, were it run by professional athletes.

Lastly, there are those who dislike the bar's monopoly on legal services. These critics usually cite the inability of some Americans to get to court because they cannot afford to hire lawyers – an increasing number of middle-class as well as poor Americans, given escalating costs and the unavailability of legal insurance. Lawyers may indeed be plentiful, runs this argument, but too few are willing to undertake *pro bono* work or accept small cases on a contingent-fee basis.

Whatever the accuracy of the criticism, law demands an expertise, painfully acquired and maintained, that few non-professionals can attain. While it is certainly true that impediments to access can lead to injustice, the increasing popularity of less-costly Alternative Dispute Resolution (ADR) services can help mitigate this problem. So could the CORE Court systems proposed in the second section of this book. Perhaps the real solution lies less in admitting everybody to the present system than in crafting satisfactory alternatives.

Americans Now Think of Lawsuits as Lotteries . . . and Tools.

There is, to be sure, nothing new about individuals seeking windfalls via lawsuits. The old canard about the victim of a minor car accident, who starts crying, "Whiplash!" even before the broken glass stops tinkling, still applies. But three things are new. One is the amount of money involved for both litigants and lawyers. A second is the expansion of the number of grievances now considered suitable for "monetized redress." And a third is the alarmingly common use of lawsuits as competitive business and political tools.

Some commentators link this phenomenon to other contemporary social issues, among them a growing unwillingness to take responsibility for one's actions, coupled with an inflated and absolutist sense of one's personal rights. Harvard Law School professor Mary Ann Glendon made this point eloquently in her 1991 book, *Rights Talk*, where she decried "our strident language of rights" and speculated on "the possibility . . . that our shallow rights talk is a faithful reflection of what our culture has become."[6]

Irresponsibility plus rights yield a simple world-view: When anything goes wrong, somebody else must pay. Other commentators, such as Charles Sykes in *A Nation of Victims*, point to the prevalent "victimization" themes of talk shows and the emphasis on "victimization" in many forms of psychotherapy.[7] Indeed, the United States may be the only country in history to elevate victimhood – not purposeful martyrdom or self-sacrifice, but mere victimization – to the stature of a moral absolute, and then to make that absolute pay off in court.

And the cult of irresponsibility is intensified, legally, by yet another curious factor. As columnist Meg Greenfield points out, today in lawsuits and other instances involving alleged misconduct (for example, rules violations in political matters), "financial settlement becomes as much a *substitute* for facing up to the misconduct as a penalty for it." [8] Thus the "victims" (real and imagined) and the "blameworthy" interact to "monetize grievance."

Yet another factor with non-legal roots may be the growing national love for (addiction to?) lotteries and other forms of gambling, which fuels irrational but powerful expectations of striking it rich. In the courtroom, this culturally-sanctioned expectation permits plaintiffs to ask for, and juries to grant, damage awards that bear no relation to the actual harm suffered. These large, unwarranted rewards set up a vicious circle. Plaintiffs can file essentially frivolous claims as a money-making endeavor, betting that defendants will pay to settle the case before trial, so as not to risk encountering a "Robin Hood" jury.

Several additional factors encourage the "lawsuit as lottery" mentality. One is human nature. The fact that most people know they will never win the lottery doesn't keep them from playing. A 1995 Justice Department survey of state court dockets in the country's 75 most populous counties found that only two percent of 762,000 cases considered were resolved by juries. Plaintiffs won 52 percent of these, but were awarded punitive damages in only six percent of those cases. The median punitive damage award was only $50,000.[9]

It is difficult to know whether surveys such as this indicate a long-term trend. What is clear is that one well-publicized megabucks settlement can, and does, spawn lawsuits in almost geometrical progression. *Liebeck v. McDonald's Restaurants,* the $3.5 million hot coffee jury award (which was later reduced during appeal), prompted similar claims against that company and various other vendors of hot foods and beverages.[10] Executives of public companies now routinely expect lawsuits to be filed immediately upon publication of any significant news about that company, whether positive or negative.

The human genome may or may not include a "lottery gene." More certain is the fact that lotteries have to be run somewhere. In recent years, rightly or wrongly, several states, including Mississippi and Alabama, have acquired reputations as good places to sue. *Business Week* reports that "Alabama's punitive-damage boom has snagged companies ranging from Ford Motor Co. to Sears, Roebuck & Co. to Prudential Insurance Co. This year

[1994] alone, Alabama juries have awarded more than $170 million in punitive damages, not including wrongful death judgments."[11]

Rural areas have also become popular sites for lawsuit casinos. According to the *Wall Street Journal,* "Plaintiffs' lawyers are going out of their way to sue big companies these days. All the way to backwaters like Plaquemine, La., Union City, Tenn., and Eutaw, Ala."[12] Small-town and rural juries may be more sympathetic to plaintiffs and generous with defendants' money, especially in class-action suits. Plaintiffs' attorneys can "shop" for state judges (many of whom are elected) with greater hopes of finding a favorable one than in a congested federal court where cases may be assigned at random. Since most large corporations do business nearly everywhere, such shopping is possible.

The results can be astounding when the locals get involved. In 1995, a Jackson, Miss., jury awarded $100 million in compensatory damages and $400 million in punitive damages to a local funeral parlor that had sued a Canadian firm for breach of contract. A few months before, a jury in Laurel, Miss., awarded $38 million in punitive damages to one auto-loan borrower who claimed he'd been overcharged.[13] That same year, two Texas lawyers were fined when they filed the same lawsuit 17 times in two days, changing only the names of the plaintiffs.[14]

Given these highly publicized outcomes, it is reasonable that some of those who focus on the "lawsuit as lottery" problem place special blame on the abuse of punitive liability and joint-and-several liability. Many jurisdictions permit juries to "punish" defendants for egregious actions by awarding monetary compensation in excess of actual damage suffered: thus the term "punitive." Joint-and-several liability is a legal theory that permits a single defendant to be held liable for the wrongdoing of other defendants, and for defendants to be assessed damages according to their ability to pay, not on the basis of what percentage of the damage they actually did.

Especially when so-called "deep pocket" (wealthy) defendants are involved, punitive damages and joint-and-several liability, plus class-action suits, have often become more like redistribution-of-wealth mechanisms than elements of justice. Says Yale University law professor George L. Priest: "'I've been studying jury verdicts for many years. It's clear that something is out of control.'"[15]

Human nature and a system gone awry. How serious has it become? What is the cost? In 1991, the *Agenda for Civil Justice Reform in America,* a report produced by the President's Council on Competitiveness, estimated that businesses and governments spend over $80 billion annually on direct litigation costs and insurance premiums, and up to $300 billion indirectly. In 1989, 18 million civil cases were filed: one for every ten adults.[16] In 1995, a study by Tillinghast-Towers Perrin, a management consulting firm, concluded that costs related to torts (legal expenses and settlements) take 2.2 percent of America's Gross Domestic Product, as compared with 0.8 percent in Britain, France and Canada, and 0.5 percent in Japan. The study estimates that legal costs have grown 50 percent faster than the economy. Although there are signs that the rate of increase is starting to slow, the real and potential drain on the economy remains higher than for any of America's major competitors.[17]

A final cost of this increase, and one not readily reducible to monetary terms, derives from the increase in politically motivated lawsuits. Some of these may have merit. The civil rights movement would have faltered without this recourse. Other suits reflect and implement an emerging political consensus on the importance of the environment, if not always a consensus on proper measures to be taken to protect it. However, in recent years a new kind of political suit, designed to intimidate, has arisen. Called "SLAPPs" –"Strategic Lawsuits against Public Participation"— the purpose of such actions is to stifle criticism and political activism, or to advance some agenda.[18] When undertaken against individuals by entities with large budgets and staff attorneys, even an entirely innocent defendant can be ruined.

The Problem Is System Overload

Finally, both the civil and criminal courts are congested. Since due process requires that criminal matters take priority over civil cases, resources must be diverted to the criminal system at the very time that the civil system needs more resources. Delays make civil cases more costly. The longer it takes to get to trial, the more opportunity for time-consuming and expensive discovery activities . . . and the greater the incentive to settle even frivolous suits out of court. Heavy burdens are placed on judges. Even the physical infrastructure is deteriorating, particularly at the federal level. Overworked people and inadequate facilities combine to degrade the quality of justice. Too much work and too little infrastructure may be frustrations primarily to those who work within and use the system, but the effects are visible to the society as a whole. They cannot be discounted.

But The Problem is Systemic

All these explanations have elements of truth. Some of the nation's most prominent attorneys have written heartfelt, thoughtful books deploring these conditions and their consequences (Mary Ann Glendon's *A Nation under Lawyers* and Sol M. Linowitz' *The Betrayed Profession* being excellent examples).[19] And all these explanations have a certain appeal. It is easy to blame the lawyers. But the lawyers – nearly a million of them expected by 2000 – did not create the demand for their services out of thin air. It is also easy to blame the increasing litigiousness of this society on greed and the lottery mentality. But these undesirable traits did not create all the new laws and regulations. Political factors and changing popular sensibilities have also been at work. The government has been increasing the demand for lawyers by regulating more and more aspects of American life. And every era seems to serve up one profession as exemplar of greed. In the 1920s and 1930s, it was stockbrokers; in the 1950s, Madison Avenue account executives; in the 1980s, investment bankers. Now, it's more often than not, the lawyers.

It is also easy to blame at least some of the clients: the people who milk the system for personal profit as well as those who use civil justice to advance political and social agendas, and to intimidate opponents. In a 1981 book, when the problem was already apparent but far less intense than today, Marlene Adler Marks noted the proliferation of reasons for suing. *The Suing of America* classified lawsuits as: Protest, Why-Me, Self-Help, Policy-Change, Greed, Vindication, Harassment, and several others.[20]

Still, in this context, the problem is not why people sue. It is how the system has come to handle the load, the growing burden of legitimate, frivolous, and predatory cases. The sad fact is, *the civil justice system, in its present form, is both dysfunctional and obsolete. Dysfunction and obsolescence make possible the other abuses, and permit those who exploit and misuse the system to make large profits from it.*

Now let's take a look at how the American legal system developed, and at why it must continue to develop and evolve to meet the needs of the 21st century.

1 See American Bar Association, Commission on Professionalism, "In the Spirit of Public Service: A Blueprint for the Rekindling of Lawyer Professionalism," Chicago: ABA, 1986.

2 Randall Samborn, "Anti-Lawyer Attitude Up," *National Law Journal,* August 9, 1993, at p. 1.

3 R. William Ide III, "Rebuilding the Public's Trust: Working towards an Improved Justice System and Renewed Respect for Lawyers," *ABA Journal,* September 1993, at p. 8.

4 "Perspectives," *Newsweek,* February 26, 1996, at p. 21.

5 *Bates v. State Bar of Arizona,* 433 U.S. 350, 97 S. Ct. 2691, 53 L. Ed. 2d 810 (1977).

6 Mary Ann Glendon, *Rights Talk: The Impoverishment of Political Discourse* (New York: Free Press, 1991) at pp. x, 172.

7 See Charles A. Sykes, *A Nation of Victims: The Decay of the American Character* (New York: Saint Martin's, 1992).

8 Meg Greenfield, "The Money Solution," *Newsweek,* February 24, 1997, at p. 82.

9 Richard C. Reuben, "Plaintiffs Rarely Win Punitives, Study Says," *ABA Journal,* October 1995, at p. 26.

10 *Liebeck v. McDonald's Restaurants,* 1995, WL 360309 (N.M. Dist. Ct. 1994).

11 "Jackpots from Alabama Juries," *Business Week,* November 28, 1994, at p. 83.

12 Richard B. Schmitt, "Justice RFD: Big Suits Land in Rural Courts," *Wall Street Journal,* October 10, 1996, at p. B-1.

13 Janet Novack, "Move over, Alabama," *Forbes,* June 17, 1996, at p. 81.

14 Hilliard Grillo, "Expensive Shopping," *National Law Journal,* November 27, 1995, at p. A-4.

15 "Jackpots from Alabama Juries," *Business Week,* November 28, 1994, at p. 83.

16 President's Council on Competitiveness, *Agenda for Civil Justice Reform: A Report from the President's Council on Competitiveness* (Washington, DC: Government Printing Office, 1991) at p. 1.

17 Gene Koretz, "Economic Trends," *Business Week,* December 4, 1995, at p. 24.

18 See George W. Pring and Penelope Canan, *SLAPPs: Getting Sued for Speaking Out* (Philadelphia: Temple University Press, 1996).

19 Mary Ann Glendon, *A Nation under Lawyers: How the Crisis in the Legal Profession Is Transforming American Society* (New York: Farrar, Straus & Giroux, 1994) and Sol. M. Linowitz, *The Betrayed Profession: Lawyering at the End of the Twentieth Century* (New York: Scribner's, 1994).

20 Marlene Adler Marks, *The Suing of America: Why and How We Take Each Other to Court* (New York: Seaview Books, 1981).

Chapter Two
Enduring Ideals and
Present Realities

I have suggested that the crisis of the civil justice system has both symptomatic and systemic aspects, and that the systemic aspects will prove the more important. To show this, it will be useful to move beyond generalities and consider the "adversary system" in more detail, especially the seemingly self-evident belief that, if two parties have at each other in a rigidly structured and impartial setting, truth and justice will emerge. This consideration will reveal that, as is so often the case in human affairs, goals and procedures can get confused.

Some of this confusion is inherent in the profession. An attorney is obligated, professionally and morally, to champion his or her client's cause. But an attorney is also an "officer of the court," exercising powers such as subpoena on behalf of society as a whole. And, increasingly, attorneys are also businesspeople with personal interests in outcomes. This is true for the "in-house" lawyers who work for corporations and the government. It is certainly true for attorneys who take large cases on a contingent-fee basis.

The vast majority of attorneys probably balance these conflicting forces ethically. However, the growing popular perception, and the increasing sense of not a few lawyers, is that the profession is no longer honorable.

A few snapshots:

A letter, written by a lawyer in response to a *Fortune Maga- zine* article about Stephen Covey's *The Seven Habits of Highly Ef- fective People.*

"Today, lawyers are actually obliged to obfuscate and distort the truth or else risk the penalties of malpractice or professional censure. Habit four, for example – 'Think win/win.' Win/win has no place in the adversary system, which allows no substi- tute for winning for one's client; the other guy is the enemy. Or take habit five about first seeking to understand, then to be un- derstood. The reality in the courtroom is that you cannot admit that the other side has a point.

"Since the bottom line of lawyering cannot be truth and jus- tice, it must be bottom-line moneymaking – so much for habit two, having a mental image of an outcome conforming to val- ues you cherish. It bothers the young lawyer for a while, but it becomes easier – like a lie: difficult at first, but with practice you hardly notice it."[1]

The comments of a college student, the son of two lawyers, on why he had abandoned his lifelong dream of becoming a lawyer after watching the O. J. Simpson trial: "We sit around the dorm and watch the trial, and almost laugh out loud at what a farce is being made of the justice system. . . . It's totally like justice can be bought. It makes you think twice about wanting to jump in and sign on."[2]

Finally, a news report in *Business Week,* worth quoting at length.

"Roy M. Cohn, the flamboyant lawyer best known as Sena- tor Joseph R. McCarthy's henchman in the 1950s, once said: 'I don't want to know what the law is. I want to know who the judge is.' The comment is as crass today as it was then. But more and more, high-priced attorneys clashing over billions of dollars live by Cohn's advice. 'I'm paid to win and to take advantage of the system,' says New York defense lawyer Dennis E. Glazer of Davis, Polk & Wardwell.

"That's exactly what Glazer recently did. In a $2.5 billion battle between airline titans Delta Air Lines, Inc., and Pan Am Corp., Glazer spearheaded an elaborate three-year strategy for Delta that entailed everything from forum-shopping to investigating judges' backgrounds. These maneuvers were neither illegal nor unethical. They merely took advantage of an imperfect, malleable system, in the process costing Delta many millions of dollars for its bevy of lawyers. And for Delta, they delivered a stunning victory in December that saved the Atlanta-based carrier from life-threatening litigation.

"What makes the Delta case so noteworthy is the tidy way every element of the legal strategy fell into place. But similar high-stakes legal maneuvering goes on everywhere. Lawyers involved in hotly contested courtroom brawls look for any possible edge over their opponents. Cases ranging from product liability to the O.J. Simpson murder trial rely on costly scientific methods to refute evidence. Jury consultants study how characteristics such as race and gender may affect a case. And lawyers search painstakingly for sympathetic legal forums. 'There didn't used to be the pressures associated with losing that there are today,' says Donald E. Vinson, a litigation-support expert. 'Today these things are all a standard part of trial advocacy.'"[3]

If this country has come to define justice as that which results from "clever maneuvering," we surely have come a long and dangerous way from our ethical and political roots.

The *American Heritage Dictionary* defines justice in part as "equitableness or moral rightness." These terms convey fairness and balance. The dictionary also defines justice as "the maintenance or administration of law." The words "victory" and "defeat" do not appear in this definition, for victory and defeat, with their all-or-nothing qualities, are often very different from justice. An equitable system is one that balances, that weighs and measures, and that applies an agreed set of social and legal principles. The symbol of justice is the scale, not the sword. True, for the parties involved, victory is to be sought, defeat avoided. But victory and defeat, and the strategies and tactics they require, are not the essence of justice. They are, or should be, techniques leading to the application of justice.

And therein lies the systemic defect that makes possible so many of the other problems and abuses. *The procedures associated with the adversary system, which were always intended to be a means to an end (the application of justice), have become an end and a force unto themselves.* Victory goes to the party best able to manipulate and employ – and further distort and suborn – a system that has gotten out of hand. To see this, it is necessary to understand how the system arose in the first place, then to look at the relationship between the present disarray and the Information Revolution now upon us.

THE ORIGIN AND NATURE OF THE ADVERSARY SYSTEM

Throughout history, there have been trials. Indeed, the administration of institutionalized justice probably antedates recorded history by millennia. Anthropology tells us that even in the first recognizably human social order – the small hunter-gatherer band – disputes arose requiring adjudication. There were, however, no universal structures for settling disputes or dealing with "criminal" acts. Custom and informal consultation resolved most disputes. Morality was self-enforcing. The man who refused to share the animal he had killed knew that, soon enough, no one would share with him. Survival required reciprocity. For those who transgressed too severely, the ultimate punishment was banishment. A solitary individual stood little chance in the wilderness.[4]

Law as an institution may have begun around 10,000 years ago, with the Neolithic Revolution. As people became farmers and started to build cities, it became possible to store wealth: first as land and goods, then as money. Opportunities for conflict increased accordingly, as did conflict in cities among people who were not intimately dependent upon each other for daily survival. Gradually, civilizations began evolving special procedures to deal with these disputes and creating special classes of officials to handle them. Sometimes these were priests or kings, sometimes merely respected elders. Gradually, judges emerged. All faced the same problem: how to determine the facts of a dispute, and then what to do to settle it.[5]

The range of dispute resolution techniques employed seems to have been limited only by imagination. There were soothsaying and divination, trial by ordeal, trial by combat, oaths and compurgations, carefully crafted formulas for determining compensation (whether money or blood), and thousands of arrangements requiring recognizable judicial proceedings of one sort or another. King Solomon provided an ancient example of judicial wisdom at work when he ordered that an infant be divided between two claimant mothers. He'd reasoned that the real mother would give the child away rather than see it killed.

Rome also knew something of lawsuits. As historian Jerome Carcopino put it: "From the reign of one emperor to another, litigation was a rising tide which nothing could stem, throwing on the public courts more work than men could muster. . . . [The Emperor] Vespasian wondered how to struggle with the flood of suits so numerous that 'the life of the advocates could scarce suffice' to deal with them.'"[6] Shakespeare, Dickens, and Mark Twain, among many others, have pondered the lawsuit as a human (or inhuman) phenomenon.

So litigation you have always with you. True enough. But only within the last century or two, and primarily within the English-speaking countries, has the notion arisen that letting the adversaries present their cases before a neutral presiding judge and passive jury was the most reliable system for determining the facts and meting out awards and punishments. Even a cursory look at the adversary system's rise will reveal just how curious and historically-contingent it was.

THE ADVERSARY SYSTEM: ITS RISE AND RATIONALE

Three things stand out about the modern adversary system. First, although many of its components date back millennia, each component had its own historical development. Second – and this is vital – the components came together in their present form to meet the needs of an emerging Industrial Age economy and society. And third, the adversary system expressed certain basic values of that emerging society. Some of these were legal: the insulation of the judge and jury from political and popular pressures, especially. But they also expressed even more fundamental beliefs in the value of the individual and his or her pursuits; in human reason and rationality; and in the pragmatic quest for resolution, as opposed to the search for absolute truth. In the end, societal values and the preservation of those values shaped the purposes of the system. The procedures and components were means to those ends, not ends in themselves.

In *The Adversary System: A Description and Defense*, legal scholar Stephan Landsman provides a superb summary of the system's development, from the Middle Ages on.[7] According to

Landsman, the first vital factor was the fading of more barbaric forms of jurisprudence, most notably trial by battle and ordeal. These were not true adversarial proceedings, since it was believed that the judgment would be rendered by God, who would cause the appropriate outcome. Evidence and argument were irrelevant. And, Landsman notes wryly, "Because the court relied on divine intervention, there was no appellate process."[8]

After the church banned clerical participation in such "trials" in 1215, the way was open for the secular jury to develop. Originally, the criminal jury and the civil "assize" were instruments of the king. Prominent locals were called to rule on disputes of which they often had personal knowledge . . . and sometimes personal prejudice. Jurors were free to gather their own evidence. Trials had no formal structure. Judgment was often arbitrary. However, in a complex process requiring half a millennium, the jury gradually evolved into a neutral and passive body, empowered to hear only the evidence presented to it.

Still, the evolution of the jury was insufficient to bring about the modern system. That required a set of concurrent evolutions in access, structure, and procedures.

The first requirement was openness. Since the courts would hear only cases brought before them, they had to be willing to adjudicate all kinds of new issues, especially as society grew more complex. This meant that the system could retain an inherent flexibility, no matter what its procedural quirks. Second, the system required new kinds of professionals. Judges changed from purely royal officers to creatures of fierce independence. Lawyers grew into practitioners, then professionals who saw themselves as both partisan advocates and defenders of higher ideals. And, given the shift from ordeal to evidence, elaborate rules had to develop for the conduct of trials, specifying what kinds of evidence were and were not admissible, and for what reasons. These specifications and limitations made it possible to give resolution priority over the search for absolute truth. And thus a point too often overlooked:

Civil justice, in its essence, is neither an endless search for truth nor a means of administering punishment. Civil justice exists primarily to resolve non-criminal disputes efficiently and equitably, in the interests of both the parties and society.

Again, all this took centuries. But even on the eve of the Industrial Revolution, the system was not yet truly adversarial. Courtroom debate was still relatively unimportant. Proceedings centered on written pleadings, which had to be done with meticulous care. The better pleading often won, regardless of the merits of the case. And witnesses were still not considered totally reliable. In fact, the so-called "party-witness rule" forbade a defendant from testifying on his or her own behalf. The rationale was that such testimony would be worthless because the defendant would lie. This exclusion had led to a form of legalized blackmail. People could make scurrilous charges against wealthy individuals (sodomy was a common accusation), knowing that the accused could not defend himself. As James Oldham, a scholar of the period, put it: "A threat to prosecute a person for a wholly fabricated offense could be used to extort money, since there was a real risk that the prosecution might succeed, especially with certain types of alleged offenses. The [alleged] victim . . . could, after all, testify, while the falsely accused defendant could not."[9] Often, it was easier to settle quietly, out of court, than face the danger and humiliation of a public proceeding, no matter how baseless the charge.

Thus, by the eve of the Industrial Revolution, many of the components of the present system were in place. But they still weren't quite working together, and major abuses and procedural impediments remained. Reforming the parts alone could not bring about the final step. The adversary system had to be "right for the times" as well.

The emerging era required a legal system that would be more open and egalitarian, more pragmatic, and more responsive to changing economic and social realities. Writes Landsman:

"The 1700s and 1800s were a time of intense social and economic ferment. They were the centuries of the American and French Revolutions and of dramatic industrialization. The traditional bases of wealth and power in English society, real property and aristocratic position, were steadily undermined by growing profits from trade and manufacture. Those who profited in the new industries swelled the ranks of the middle class. . . .

"The demise of stability led to a new legal situation. The numbers and sorts of disputes that were brought to the courts grew significantly. Amidst all the conflict and change it is likely that a desire arose for a legal mechanism that could meet the problems of the day and yet preserve some continuity with the more stable past. The adversary system met these requirements. It was an outgrowth of procedures that had been used for hundreds of years in England and America. The idea of a neutral and passive fact finder was not a radical departure, but rather the extension of trusted and traditional methods. At the same time, the adversary courts were receptive to new claims. They allowed the parties to define the issues and the evidence. They thereby provided a forum for questions that no other institution in society would hear or resolve. . . .

". . . adversary procedure was the right procedure for the times. It did not pose a threat of radical change, but could credibly accommodate the demands of the forces of change at work in England and America."[10]

The legal needs of the Industrial Age were obvious: to create a set of standardized procedures and a rational, relatively predictable body of law that could handle the requirements of the citizenry in an era of burgeoning industry and commerce. Early capitalist ventures had enough difficulty surviving brutal competition and the vicissitudes of the business cycle. An arbitrary, capricious, tradition-encrusted legal system could make business nearly impossible. Moreover, the system had to focus on getting results, not ferreting out the truth at any cost or kowtowing to outmoded social arrangements.

But why an adversary system? The answer is simply that its elements were already in place; that it worked; and that it appealed to the philosophical underpinnings of the era. The Enlightenment placed great value on the powers of the human mind, of thought unfettered by coercion or privilege. The neutral judge and jury fit. New and more precise rules of evidence and procedure also reflected this passion. Further, it was felt that two parties, contending as equals, using rational powers of persuasion and able to cross-examine witnesses freely, could enable the jury to get at the facts. Perhaps not always as well as some Grand Inquisitor with time on his hands or local squire with authority to protect, but well enough to produce tolerable, dependable, and predictable justice.

So the final touches were added and refined, first in English law before the American Revolution, then in the adaptations of an industrializing, expanding America. Trials would now center on the presentation of evidence. Defendants could testify. Witnesses would be subject to vigorous cross-examination, in accordance with strict rules of evidence. The courtroom would become an isolated universe of pure legal and procedural rationality, freed from outside pressures and knowing only what the rules permitted it to know.

As a structure, the modern adversary system is a combination of three elements. Each, in theory, upholds certain basic principles. To summarize, these are:

- Parties-in-interest: The right of people to seek dispute resolution and justice, and their corresponding right to be actively involved in developing and presenting evidence to the judge and jury who will resolve the dispute. The principles upheld here are the sovereignty and rights of the individual, and society's trust that inquisitorial methods are unnecessary.

- Decision-makers: The use of a judge and jury who are neutral and passive – in a sense, intelligent machines registering and analyzing data – so that the evidence presented by the parties will be the only factual information used to decide the outcome of the parties' dispute. The principle here is that justice requires absolute neutrality and impartiality, which is possible to reasoning creatures.

- Procedures: The use of intricate sets of rules, i.e., the Rules of Evidence, the Rules of Procedure, and professional ethical rules and codes of conduct, to govern the behavior of the parties and their lawyers in developing and presenting evidence to the jury and judge. The principles here are, again, faith in instrumental rationality, plus pragmatism.

And thus the rise and rationale of the modern adversary system. It all seems so obvious that it's hard to believe that it came together only a couple of centuries ago. It all seems (to borrow a good Enlightenment word) "self-evident." Of course, people should have the right to bring their own cases and present their evidence with the aid of counsel. Of course, judges and juries should be neutral and passive. Of course, clear and rational rules and procedures are necessary. But it also is starting to become self-evident that this system, like those which preceded it, now suffers from its share of abuses and shortcomings. And indeed, it may well be that the present adversary system now undermines the very principles it was established to protect.

THE ADVERSARY SYSTEM: REALITY

No one has ever claimed that the adversary system is perfect. Legal scholars have produced an extensive and impressive critical literature. Many regard it as the legal world's equivalent of Winston Churchill's characterization of democracy: the worst form of government, save for all the other kinds. Others, while not denying its faults, defend it passionately. On the whole, scholars and lawyers have agreed that the adversary system's virtues outweigh its disadvantages.

Landsman expresses the consensus when he argues that, because the adversary system emphasizes individuality and rights, because it lets the litigants (rather than the judge and jury) control the presentation and development of evidence, it best suits a democracy. "Adversary procedure," he writes, "has served as a guardian of individual liberty since its inception. It has facilitated the extension of personal rights to a wide range of minority groups. Given these facts and the absence of a clearly superior alternative, the American commitment to the adversary system ought to be maintained."[11]

Landsman is correct. The adversary system should be maintained. *But not the present adversary system.* The time has come to question whether the adversary system in its current condition any longer guarantees either rights or fairness. This is not to say that the system never did. Far from it . But it is possible to imagine many real-world variants of the theoretical system.

To repeat: The present system is the product of a particular era, with its own requirements. In many important ways our needs are different from theirs. And their reforms have given rise to our dysfunctions and abuses.

To see this, it is necessary to go back over the three components of the present system, and to determine whether the realities still reflect the theories. Unfortunately, even a cursory examination reveals the divergence of theory from reality. To put it simply, none of these elements works as intended anymore. And the system as a whole has been captured and suborned by the abuses that its elements now make possible, sanction, and reward.

Element 1

Theory: The parties-in-interest are actively involved in their cases.

Practice: In my years as a general counsel for three publicly-held companies, I have often been in the position of hiring firm lawyers to represent the corporation. I have been struck repeatedly by the expectation of these lawyers that they will, in essence, take over the case. On one occasion, when I asked a lawyer how he felt about in-house counsel's involvement in developing strategy, he was actually offended. "I'm sorry," he told me. "We cannot work under those conditions. When we take on a case, we intend to win it. Our own reputation is at stake, meaning we must be able to make all the strategic decisions."

In other words, my company, the actual party-in-interest, was expected to take directions from an outside lawyer, lest we harm his reputation. Whether this lawyer's approach was in *our* best interest mattered hardly at all.

This was not an isolated instance. Routinely, parties to cases are reduced to mere pawns in a chess game played by lawyers. Further, because of the contingent-fee system, many attorneys now have financial as well as professional interests in pulling off the big one. In the now infamous McDonald's hot coffee case, the woman initially sought only $2,000 for the medical costs, plus her daughter's wages for the three weeks of work she'd missed while caring for her mother. By the time the attorney prepared the complaint, however, the demand had grown to $100,000 compensatory damages, plus triple punitive damages. One need not possess a particularly vivid imagination to guess how it happened.[12]

Unfortunately, clients today routinely defer to their lawyers. Part of this is normal. The client, seeking expertise he or she does not possess, generally expects to follow the professional's recommendations. But what should a client do, when told by her lawyers that a $2,000 claim should be multiplied two hundred fold . . . for starters? Parties-in-interest too often seem to lose all common sense as they stand by and watch their lawyers take actions that might hit the jackpot, but are also contrary to the client's other wishes and interests. It is not uncommon, for example, for lawyers to advise their clients to reject settlements that the client might consider acceptable. Nor is it uncommon for a lawyer to construct a legal theory of a case and then, while preparing his or her client for testimony, to coach, or remind, the client as to the relationship between the facts of the case and that legal theory, helping the client to know which facts to emphasize and which to minimize.

These practices are neither illegal nor exactly improper. Ethically, an attorney must give the client the best possible representation, within the rules. But today, personal pressures – reputation and money, especially – can push the lawyer toward telling the best possible story for the client rather than the client's best possible story. The distinction is subtle but profound. Or perhaps, not so subtle. It is the difference between crafting the case and adopting a scorched earth/take-no-prisoners strategy. As one commentator puts it: Many lawyers now believe that being a zealous advocate "REQUIRES the assertion of every conceivable right or arguable position without regard to their private knowledge or opinions as to the truth or validity of a claim and the likely consequences of such advocacy."[13]

Of course, it's easy to shrug this off with "Money and reputation, so what else is new?" But few non-lawyers now realize the extent to which these pressures have been intensified by institutionalized changes in the profession and its practice. The contingent-fee system, once reserved for meritorious clients who were too poor to afford the hourly fee system, has evolved into a perpetual money-making machine. Once, the contingent-fee system was ethically acceptable because it aided people of modest means, and because the amounts involved were also modest. It was never intended to provide a comfortable-to-outrageous livelihood for thousands of attorneys.

Meanwhile, the hourly fee system has also been subjected to escalating abuse. Of course, there is nothing new about making the work fit the available hours. But the very complexity and longevity of modern lawsuits have become the major source of huge legal bills. *The Wall Street Journal* quotes one defense attorney concerning his opposition to tort reform: "We in the defense bar have earned a living defending these cases. . . . Were they to dry up, we would lose another source of income."[14]

Again: So what else is new? But law is a profession, where other considerations accompany, and must sometimes override, the need to make a profit. A doctor who publicly opposed medical research on the grounds that it would cut down the number of sick patients would probably not augment either his practice or his reputation by that statement. Why should analogous behaviors be tolerated from lawyers?

Perhaps it's because reputation has also changed its nature. In the old days, before lawyers could solicit business openly and aggressively ("Dial 1-800-WHY HURT," invites one now-legendary personal injury ad), reputation was a vital form of advertising. But reputation centered on ethics, intelligence, diligence, and service to clients, not income *per se*. Today, publications such as the *National Law Journal* and the *American Lawyer* publicly rank lawyers and law firms by size and number of verdicts won and overall revenues.

In this media-saturated society, people learn about people and events they themselves haven't experienced by sometimes inaccurate entertainment. In this case, though, TV and the movies may be offering an uncomfortably accurate portrayal of some aspects of the legal profession. In lawyer-centered novels, TV series, and films, attorneys are routinely described as "you know, the one who got that zillion dollar settlement in the Rubber Ducky case." And everybody nods.

Finally, the Law of Supply and Demand works both ways. Demand for lawyers increases their numbers. But as the number of lawyers has grown, so has the competition for clients. Lawyers who win have always gotten clients. But now the pressure is to win big, and publicly. Perhaps a *Wall Street Journal* cartoon captured this new sensibility and this new imperative best, when it showed an announcer standing in front of the judge's bench, pointing to a waving attorney. The caption: "In this corner, fighting for the defense, winner of over 200 lawsuits, last year's most valuable attorney . . ."[15]

The lawyer-client relationship has corroded for another reason. Sometimes it's hard, if not impossible, to know who the client is. Enter the class-action lawsuit. Under Rule 23 of the Rules of Civil Procedure, a large number of plaintiffs with essentially the same claim may form a "class." This procedure has a double logic. It's valuable for plaintiffs whose individual claims may be too small to warrant expensive litigation, and it keeps the courts from having to try essentially the same case over and over.

However, attorneys often undertake class-action cases for a percentage of any damages awarded, similar to the contingent-fee system for individual clients. This leads to a pernicious result. *The attorney generally has a far greater financial interest in the outcome than any individual party-in-interest.*

As one federal court decision (*In Re Oracle Securities*) has described the situation:

"In class actions, however, class counsel run the litigation with little or, more realistically, no input from their clients since the class members generally have relatively small individual claims which give them insufficient incentive to supervise their lawyers. When the prospect of settlement arises, the unique dynamics of the lawyer/client relationship in class actions raise particular problems. An attractive attorney fee provision in the settlement may induce class counsel to settle regardless of the likelihood that further pursuit of litigation might substantially increase the total class recovery."[16]

This has been a special problem in securities litigation, where the lawyer often actually initiates the case by getting someone (sometimes a friend, employee, or family member) to buy stock in a company and become the named plaintiff for the purpose of suing the company on behalf of all shareholders.

In some cases, the class-action lawsuit becomes little more than a speculative commercial endeavor. Class-action defendants know that a primary purpose of the suits is to generate cash for the lawyers. So serious has the situation become that, according to the *New York Times*, "A growing number of companies, desperate to limit their exposure to potentially ruinous litigation, are initiating class-action lawsuits *against themselves,*" in order to negotiate settlements that could apply to future contingencies.[17] This gets the money in the hands of the lawyers while avoiding the costs and agonies of extended litigation.

And it's all legal, so long as the Rule 23 procedures are followed. The lawyers get their cash with minimal interference from the putative plaintiffs. In short, class-action has evolved from a legal convenience to, in essence, the realm of the "plaintiffless lawsuit."

What makes this work for the lawyers is the reality of heavy defense costs and the high risk of erratic and unduly large jury verdicts. Many defendants – especially "deep pocket" corporations – find it cheaper, and therefore in at least the short-term interests of their shareholders, to settle even the most meritless class-action claims. Thus, just the threat of the lawsuit can generate significant revenues for the lawyers making the threat. A 1993 study of shareholder class-action settlements by National Economic Research Associates, Inc., concluded that the merits of the case were actually less important in determining outcome than the "availability of assets" for settlement.[18]

In criminal law, this is known as extortion. In civil law, it returns us to the same kind of abuse that the adversary system was supposed to remove – the legalized blackmail associated with the "party-witness rule" in England.

Moreover, courts are often reluctant to exercise their discretion to challenge these coerced results, in part because once the contending attorneys agree, there is often no one left to present the judge with evidence of an improper settlement. As the *Oracle* decision stated, "Courts are frequently faced with the situation . . . in which one or both sides have little incentive to put forth their best case. Class counsel's memoranda in support of the settlement, for example, are replete with concessions about the weakness of their case. Given that lawyers have taken such a non-adversarial posture, it is difficult for the court to perceive the true merits of each side's potential arguments. As there is no manifest indication that the parties have not dealt with the court in good faith, however, the court has no choice but to evaluate the evidence as it has actually been presented."[19]

Connoisseurs of the ironic must find the phrase "non-adversarial posture" a special treat.

Interestingly, these and other settlements actually undermine the system in another way. Every aspect of the adversary system, from the way documents are drafted to the rights and duties of the parties under discovery and the roles of the attorneys, is built around the presumption that there will be a final showdown in court. There are no reliable statistics to indicate what percentage of cases filed actually ended up in court a hundred, or even fifty years ago. Even today, it's hard to get complete statistics. But it appears that over 90 percent of all litigation is concluded, usually by agreement of the parties, before a decision at trial.[20]

What does this mean? It can signify that the vast majority of cases don't need to go through all those adversary system procedures at all. Rational people, even aggrieved and argumentative rational people, can find less litigious ways of settling their disputes. Or it can mean that the vast majority of these cases end when one side *succumbs to the procedural assault of the other*. Most likely, both are true, although it is impossible to estimate the ratio of satisfaction to intimidation. But why rely so heavily on a complex and expensive adversary system if the parties rarely go before the official decision-makers to have their dispute resolved, or when procedures intended to guarantee fairness become weapons that keep cases from getting to the judge and jury?

There are, then, two initial good reasons for rethinking and re-engineering the present system. First, a system meant to serve the parties-in-interest now serves chiefly the lawyers via a perversion of justice that permits attorneys to over-emphasize process rather than address substance. And second, systems that respond to and enhance the human ability to reach agreement can provide justice better, faster, and cheaper. Of these, I will have more to say later.

Element 2

Theory: The judge and jury are neutral and passive, rational, and competent.

Practice: In a cartoon that appeared in several newspapers around the country in December 1994, a woman is holding two clothes hangers in front of her husband. On one hanger there is a rather frilly dress, on the other a business-like skirt and jacket. The cartoon's caption: "Which do you like better, the jury consultant's choice or the focus group's choice?"[21]

That cartoon captures much of what has gone wrong with the second element of the adversary system in modern practice. Many attorneys, instead of accepting and valuing neutral and passive juries and judges, do everything they can to avoid them. Armed with the insights and pseudo-insights of social and behavioral sciences, and focused on winning at all costs, they seek to exploit the real and presumed biases and other baggage of decision-makers whose greatest value is, according to theory, their neutrality. The theoretical construct of objectivity remains, but the reality has been reversed.

Over the last decade, an entirely new industry of "trial consultants" has arisen to help lawyers uncover and manipulate the biases of jurors. These consultants often work in teams, providing expertise in market research, opinion polling, the psychology of persuasion, and statistical analysis. Their services include focus groups, mock trials, shadow trials, witness preparation, and design of charts, videos, and other demonstrative evidence. As an ad for one such service proclaims: "Understanding jurors and what motivates them is our business. . . What are their attitudes? Their hot buttons? Their key issues? Our research will tell you."

The techniques used by these consultants have been well-honed in other endeavors, from retail sales to retail politics. Legal focus group studies now parallel other marketing techniques. A typical legal study might gather a representative group of local citizens from the area in which a case is to be tried. The group listens to a presentation that simulates what the attorneys might say in the trial. Social scientists then conduct interviews. Responses are analyzed for trends. Did the women respond more favorably than the men? Businesspeople or housewives? Whites or blacks? The attorney then uses this information to decide which prospective jurors to challenge and how to "market" the case to the actual jury.

Similarly, a trial consultant might use a shadow jury to analyze the progress of a trial. A shadow jury is a group of citizens, selected because of their resemblance to the real jurors, who are paid to sit through a trial and submit to interviews after each day's testimony. The consultants then try to determine, on a real-time basis, which hot buttons are getting pushed (or disconnected). The lawyers can then make the necessary adjustments.

Jeffrey Abramson, in *We, the Jury*, suggests that if scientific jury selection and analysis efforts are as effective as the consultants proclaim, "then facts and evidence play a subordinate role in trials." He points out that jury consultants justify their services on the grounds that they are not illegal. But this, he feels, is inadequate. The rules of the game may not have been broken, but the spirit has. "Of course, the rules of the game used to seem relatively fair: neither side could seriously outguess the other about the best and worst jurors. The frightening message today is that science can rig the game without breaking the rules – if you have enough money to spend." [22]

Mr. Abramson's personal view is that these techniques are not as effective as advertised. Nonetheless, they do have an impact. Litigants have been known to settle when advised by a trial consultant that focus groups or mock trials reveal likely bias among potential jurors, regardless of the facts. But Mr. Abramson also concludes that the trial consultant industry is symptomatic of more than tactical ruthlessness. As he writes:

"Scientific jury selection grew out of, and in turn pushed farther, the prevailing skepticism about juries as impartial institutions of justice. More than any other idea over the last generation, it captured the basic shift in our conception of the jury – from a group that would find common ground above individual differences to a group that divides, almost predictably, along all the fissures of identity in America."[23]

The notion that jury deliberation is more about partiality and politics than objectivity and evidence is also reflected in how litigators prepare for trial. Today, litigators are taught that trials can be won on form, not substance. Once, precisely wrought pleadings carried the day – and led to the substance-over-form campaigns that marked the beginning of the modern adversary system. Now theories and styles do what those arcane pleadings did: make facts secondary. True, the importance of lawyerly skills is hardly new. But the openly-acknowledged sense that trials are essentially competitive theater is unprecedented. Indeed, it is not uncommon for modern-day litigators to consult with actors and directors as well as social scientists. A 1995 Washington State legal education seminar flyer featured presentations by a playwright (strategy), an artistic director (orchestrating the trial), and an actor (communicating persuasively). The flyer was headlined, "2ⁿᵈ Annual Trial as Theater." Evidence now clearly and unabashedly takes second place behind winning the hearts of the jury. As one experienced litigator sadly confesses: "[S]olid legal representation consists more than ever of mind-reading and performing. . . . Lawyering, the art and craft, is becoming, far too often, the fast sell."[24]

In addition to the trial consultants, attorneys now have access to a veritable horde of experts. Some work on a fee basis – money for testimony favorable to the client. These experts, whatever their credentials, are often mere hired-guns. Peter Huber, author of *Galileo's Revenge,* describes one expert-referral bureau that advertises: "'If the first doctor we refer doesn't agree with your legal theory, we'll provide you with the name of a second.' This inevitably corrupts both law and science."[25] Other such experts may have their own political, cultural, and social agendas to advance.

In sum, underlying the use of trial consultants and experts (not to mention all those glitzy trial props) is an insidious view of jurors as inherently biased, ignorant, and impressionable. This view may be partially due to a belief that the unemployed, housewives, and low-end workers are more likely to serve on juries, i.e., that the better educated and more successful are likely to be excused. It may also be due to a certain arrogance among lawyers who do not see themselves as "peers" of the jury. Regardless of cause, the consequence is that this country is fast losing its respect for the jury system.[26]

This view of jurors as inherently and unavoidably biased, ignorant, and malleable is also at odds with the fundamental theoretical justification for the jury system. Since the earliest days of English law, jurors were not presumed, and were never intended to be, "ignorant." It is one thing to have no personal knowledge of the case under consideration. It is quite another to be without the minimal intellectual and cultural tools necessary to do the vital job of evaluating the evidence presented by the contending parties. For lawyers actively to seek out such persons is an affront to the system.

In this context, it is relevant that the requirement that juries be selected from a "cross section of the community" is only about thirty years old. Prior to this, juries were often selected on a more discriminatory basis, i.e., excluding women, African Americans and other minorities. Congress in 1968, and the Supreme Court in 1975, mandated more representative jury pools. The purpose was both to remedy systemic discrimination and to bring certain types of hitherto excluded "knowledge" into the system. There is no question that this change, which further democratized the jury process, was good and valuable. But, as Jeffrey Abramson points out, in the aftermath of this change, we now often expect jurors to vote as representatives of their respective communities rather than as individuals considering the evidence alone and judging on the basis of common principles.[27]

If in fact the jury system has been seriously weakened by consultants, hired-gun experts and the perversion of the cross-section requirement, is it still reasonable to believe in the existence of the "neutral and passive jury"? Or has the system become a charade? Consider the following example, reported in the *Wall Street Journal* in November 1994.

A plaintiffs' lawyer, intending to bring a class-action against Prudential Securities, filed in a small Texas border town. The lawyer reasoned that the local populace, overwhelmingly poor and uneducated, constituted "a jury pool [that] almost always favors the plaintiff" over "a big, remote company." In addition, this lawyer associated as local counsel a person who had been one of the biggest contributors to the presiding judge's election campaign. When queried, the lawyer responded that he was discharging his ethical duty of providing zealous representation for his clients by finding the most favorable forum. This was lawful in Texas.[28]

To repeat: We have come full-circle. Many components of the adversary system, originally crafted to correct an array of systemic flaws that led to systemic injustice, are now the source of injustice. Any individual juror or jury may be honest and conscientious. But the system is dysfunctional. And technically it's all ethically OK – proof, once again, of the old adage that the real scandal is not what's illegal. The real scandal is what the law lets you get away with.

Element 3

Theory: Rules of procedure, evidence, and ethics facilitate a fair presentation of evidence to the judge and jury.

Practice: Instead of assuring fairness in litigation, these rules have become a source of dysfunction and injustice. Instead of shielding litigants from procedural abuses, they have become the source of abuses. Today, rules are used as weapons in what one study has called "a war of attrition in which the goal is to harass an opponent until he capitulates because of cost, delay, or exasperation."[29]

Two rules have lent themselves especially well to abuse. The first is Rule 26 of the Federal Rules of Civil Procedure (and its counterparts in various state rules), which provides for extremely broad pre-trial discovery. The second is Rule 1.3 of the American Bar Association's Model Rules of Professional Conduct (and its counterparts in the states), concerning the lawyer's responsibility to provide zealous representation to clients. This Rule provides that: "A lawyer shall act with reasonable diligence and promptness in representing a client."

No quibbles there. But Comment 1 to the Rule provides that "A lawyer . . . may take whatever lawful and ethical measures are required to vindicate a client's cause or endeavor. A lawyer should act with commitment and dedication to the interests of the client and with zeal in advocacy upon the client's behalf." Today, many lawyers use this as justification for "scorched earth" tactics, while ignoring the second part of the rule, which states: "However, a lawyer is not bound to press for every advantage that might be realized for a client." In law, as in the military, there is a fundamental difference between the ethical professional and the amoral mercenary.

How serious is this abuse of procedure? A few years ago, the Western District of Washington, through an advisory group, conducted an extensive survey of area attorneys. The purpose was to fulfill the mandate of the 1990 Civil Justice Reform Act, which directed federal judicial districts to devise plans for reducing delays and costs of litigation. According to the study, "an overwhelming number of attorneys surveyed blamed attorneys for the problems." Specifically, they cited "(1) attorneys who seek discovery [demanding information from the other side] of insignificant or unnecessary information; (2) attorneys who use discovery to increase the cost and/or burden of litigation for opponents; and (3) attorneys who unreasonably resist discovery."[30]

Such results probably typify the nation as a whole. Other studies have found that between 65 and 75 percent of the cost of litigation derives from discovery.[31]

Running up the opponent's tab is not hard. Discovery essentially involves three procedures: interrogatories, depositions, and document subpoenas. Each is vulnerable to deliberate and extensive abuse.

A few definitions. Interrogatories are written questionnaires that demand written responses from the other side. A set of interrogatories can include a wide range of questions. Under Rule 26, the only limitation is that the questions be "relevant to the subject matter involved in the pending action," and not necessarily admissible in court as evidence. Depositions involve asking questions in person. A party can demand that adverse party or non-party witnesses appear to be questioned under oath. Neither judge nor jury is present for deposition questioning, and questions need only be "relevant." Finally, document subpoenas are used to demand written materials. Again, the criterion is relevance, broadly construed, and not admissibility.

The potential for "weaponizing" is obvious, but the actual personal and economic costs have to be experienced to be believed. So must the attitudes of some attorneys who play this game. I once dealt with a lawyer who, shortly after bringing a purported class-action lawsuit against my client, convened a "settlement meeting." He explained how much time, effort, and money we would save if we settled at once. If not, the expenditures would be enormous. He also advised us that, if we proceeded, it would be necessary for him to depose the most senior officers of my client, perhaps for several days each. When we suggested that perhaps he was more interested in a shakedown than a lawsuit, the lawyer merely smiled.

We told him that we believed the client had done nothing wrong and therefore had no interest in settling the case. The ordeal began. We received hundreds of pages of interrogatories to answer, subpoena requests for literally millions of pages of documents, as well as for all computer records, including employee e-mail. As threatened, the attorney issued deposition requests for many employees, including the most senior officers.

It cost several million dollars to process these requests, not to mention the "soft costs" of lost employee time. My client remained firm and ultimately prevailed in the case, but today many companies know that it is cheaper and less stressful to pay those millions to an extorting attorney. Extorting attorneys know it, too.

This abuse has been decades in the making. As far back as 1980, Supreme Court Justice Lewis Powell wondered whether "empirical evidence would demonstrate that untrammeled discovery actually contributes to the just resolution of disputes."[32] At the time, he was questioning Supreme Court approval of amendments liberalizing discovery rules. Three years later, after further amendment, members of the Supreme Court-appointed Rules Advisory Committee admitted that the new latitude was being misused. Still, they continued to support broad discovery powers, adding to the 1983 amendments language that authorized judges to become more active in the discovery process. Nonetheless, they warned courts "not to deprive a party of discovery that is reasonably necessary to afford a fair opportunity to develop and prepare the case."[33] In practice, only the most utterly egregious misuses tend to be addressed by the courts.

Again, the problem is the disconnection between abstract values and real-world implementation. In theory, Rule 26 buttresses the most fundamental part of the adversary system: allowing the litigants to develop their own cases. Without broad discovery, such development could never occur. With broad discovery, parties can tell a better, more complete story at trial. But today, as noted, only a small percentage of lawsuits ever come to trial. Discovery has taken on a life of its own as a way of *preventing and bypassing* the courtroom, and as a weapon of intimidation and outright extortion. Under these circumstances, the most ruthless side has the advantage.

Further – and this is crucial – the escalating abuse of discovery is made possible by the technologies of the global economy and the Information Age. Ironically, big business and small entrepreneurial firms are especially vulnerable. Large corporations present the most lucrative targets. The bigger the business, the more widely scattered are its offices and employees, the more complex its procedures, the wider its contacts. This makes it excruciatingly difficult to respond to discovery requests. The reader can well imagine what it might take to comply with a discovery request for "all documents discussing your business plans for the last five years" when that request hits a company with 20,000 employees at 50 office and manufacturing sites on three continents – a company possessed of thousands of computers, filing systems, and other archives. Conversely, a new company may have less material in the archives, but may be terribly vulnerable to the monetary costs and to the loss of employee time at a critical period in the company's development.

Still, given the likelihood that the request would produce "relevant" information, few courts would be willing to find it unreasonable.

So what should a company do? Suspend operations and spend millions to comply, or settle?

Clearly, Information Age technologies have greatly increased the amount of material to be discovered. These same technologies have also made it easier for lawyers to "throw in the kitchen sink" when drafting requests. In *The Litigation Explosion,* Walter Olson explains:

"These [interrogatory] questionnaires can take minutes to draft and weeks to answer. On one side a fifteen-dollar-an-hour paralegal downloads the questions from a disk of standardized 'pattern interrogatories'; on the other a team of top lawyers is scrambling to draft a response after an exhaustive file search and discussions with [company employees]. . . . The requesting lawyer may have to pay minor copying costs, but otherwise there is not much reason to go easy on the adversary; an extra hundred pages of responses, thumbed through in an idle moment, might yield a welcome nugget. In one big securities case, a set of interrogatories 381 pages long was served; 150,000 pages of deposition and testimony transcripts were prepared in the same case. Formbooks and disks bring this kind of imposition within the reach of the humblest lawyer: one of today's compendiums of 'pattern interrogatories' for filing in medical malpractice cases goes on for 955 densely packed pages."[34]

Finally, increased complexity and specialization expand discovery. Interrogatories become longer and harder to answer. The number of witnesses called for deposition increases, as does the amount of time required to depose them. Even when only ethical and principled attorneys are involved, discovery can now take months and years. And the longer and more costly the process becomes, the more one returns to Justice Powell's question. Whatever the theoretical justification for liberal discovery, is justice really being served? And does "zealous advocacy" – another self-evident good in the abstract – really serve the client when the measure of "zealous" is how much harassment and pain one attorney can inflict upon another's client? As one experienced litigator puts it:

"So we spend our days fighting about nothing at great expense, and we act out. I have personally witnessed otherwise sensible, highly compensated adult attorneys fighting about what the word 'mean' means, about whether a lawyer screaming during a deposition was or was not standing up while doing so, and about the crucial distinction between 'hollering' and 'raising my voice.' I have constantly found it useful to assess disputes based upon how I think a 9-year-old might react. These incidents are not limited to instances of tension or emotion getting the best of us. *The system is hard-wired to generate disputes of no lasting significance.*"[35]

It is also hard-wired to hurt people. Unlike doctors, attorneys have no "First, do no harm" ethic. Writes Olson: "America is the litigious society it is because American lawyers wield such unparalleled powers of imposition. No other country gives a private lawyer such a free hand to select a victim, tie him up in court on undefined charges, force him to hire lawyers of his own at dire expense, trash his privacy through we-have-ways-of-making-you-talk discovery, wear him down on the perpetual-motions treadmill, libel him grossly in documents that become permanent public records, and keep him scrambling to respond to Gyro Gearloose experts and Game of the States conflict theories. Other countries let lawyers or litigants do some of these things, but never with such utter impunity."[36]

Whatever else may be said of this system, it is not what its crafters intended.

SUMMARY

The present adversarial system has been corrupted and is being devastated by process run amok. In theory, the rules of procedure, evidence, and ethics play only a supporting role, helping to set up and flesh out a fair contest between the adversaries, so that the merits of the case will become clear to the judge and jury. But to the extent that these rules and procedures are now used to harass, intimidate, and carry out a war of attrition against the adverse party, the rules become the substance of the case. This mocks the intent of the adversary system, which requires that the fight be secondary to the merits.

There are essentially three reasons for why we have come to allow process to trump substance in the adversary system. First, we do not yet fully appreciate the extent of the misalignment of tools and tasks within today's legal system. These tools – especially the Rules of Procedure – were designed with courtroom use in mind, but increasingly are used and exploited for the purpose of reaching out-of-court settlements. In manufacturing, when a tool is not fitted to the task, the results are inefficiency, high cost, and usually an inferior product. In the legal context, the tools/tasks mismatch generates a troubling sense of chronic unfairness and injustice as well as more palpable costs and inefficiencies.

The second factor is changes within the legal profession, which in turn reflect changes in the larger culture. Law, like the larger society, has been coarsened. Win-at-any-cost is now the norm. This, too, encourages the abuse of procedures originally intended to guarantee fairness.

The final reason is that the volume of potentially relevant information and the complexity of the issues under dispute have grown far beyond what the crafters of the present system could have envisioned. Procedures that were well-adapted to the Industrial Age have become outdated in the Information Age.

Any of these reasons is sufficient to suggest the need for serious rethinking. Taken together, they constitute nothing less than a mandate for fundamental change. Not in the rights that the system must protect: These are lasting. Nor in the essence of the adversary system: That is still valid. Rather, there must be a restructuring and realignment of tools and tasks within the system. The old tools of dispute resolution must be recalibrated; new ones must be added. Substance, not process, must once again determine outcomes. Unless this happens, the purpose of law – the rendering of justice – and the practice of law will continue to deteriorate, and popular respect for both will continue to erode.

In short, there are now tremendous and damaging gaps between the contemporary legal system, which we call an adversary system, and that system as it should be. The present system is simply too adversarial. The system as it should be uses adversarial procedures for a greater good: the maintenance of society's laws and values through the fair and predictable resolution of its disputes. The challenge is to restore the essence of the adversarial system, so that it can again reliably provide the foundation for that greater good.

1 Letter to *Fortune*, March 6, 1995, at p. 52.

2 "Law Schools See Sharp Decline in Applicants," *Wall Street Journal*, February 17, 1995 at p. B-1.

3 Linda Himelstein, "How Delta Flew Circles around Pan Am in Court," *Business Week*, February 20, 1995, at p. 68.

4 An interesting treatment of "law" in hunter-gatherer groups is found in Kalman Glantz and John Pearce, *Exiles from Eden: Psychotherapy from an Evolutionary Perspective* (New York: Norton, 1989).

5 See, for example, Richard D. Schwartz and James C. Miller, "Legal Evolution and Societal Complexity," *American Journal of Sociology* 70 (March 1964), at pp. 159-169.

6 Quoted in Jethro K. Lieberman, *The Litigious Society* (New York: Basic Books, 1981), at p. 3.

7 Stephan Landsman, *The Adversary System: A Description and Defense* (Washington, DC: American Enterprise Institute, 1984) at pp. 7-25.

8 Ibid, at p. 9.

9 James Oldham, "Truth-Telling in the Eighteenth Century English Courtroom," *Law and History Review* 12 (Spring 1994), at p. 107.

10 Stephan Landsman, *Readings on Adversarial Justice: The American Approach to Adjudication* (St. Paul: West Publishing Co., 1988), at pp. 19-21.

11 Ibid p. 39.

12 Aric Press, "Are Lawyers Burning America?" *Newsweek,* March 20, 1995, at p. 32

13 Michael Josephson, "Going beyond the Code," *Ethics* 23/24 (Winter 1993), at p. 48.

14 Amy Stevens, "Lawyers and Clients: Corporate Clients, Some Lawyers Differ on Litigation Reform," *Wall Street Journal*, March 17, 1995, at p. B-10.

15 "Pepper . . . and Salt," *Wall Street Journal*, August 18, 1995, at p. A-9.

16 See *In Re Oracle Securities Litigation,* United States District Court of California, No. C-90-0931, August 9, 1993. Reported at Par. 98, 174, CCH Federal Securities Law Reports, 1994. Quote at par. 99, 197.

17 Barry Meier, "Lawsuits to End All Lawsuits," *New York Times,* January 10, 1996, at p. C-1. Italics added.

18 See F. Dunbar and V. Juneja, *Recent Trends II: What Explains Settlement in Shareholder Class Actions?* National Economic Research Associates, Inc., White Plains, New York, October 1993.

19 *Oracle* Case, at par. 99, 201.

20 For example, in 1986, only 6.6 percent of cases filed in federal trial courts were terminated by trial. See Terence Dungworth and Nicholas Pace,

Statistical Overview of Civil Litigation in the Federal Courts, RAND Institute for Civil Justice, 1990. In the Western District of Washington, approximately 95 percent of civil cases never go to trial. See *Professionalism Task Force Interim Report,* Federal Bar Association, Western District of Washington, December 1994, at p. 7.

21 Jim Borgman, *Cincinnati Inquirer,* reprinted in "Views," *New York Times,* December 15, 1994, at p. E-4.

22 Jeffrey Abramson, *We, the Jury: The Jury System and the Ideal of Democracy* (New York: Basic Books, 1994), at p. 154.

23 Ibid, at p. 176.

24 Anonymous, "A Litigator's Lament," *American Lawyer,* December 1993, at p. 80.

25 Peter Huber, "Expert Evidence," in *A Plan to Improve America's System of Civil Justice* (Washington, DC: National Legal Center for the Public Interest, 1992), at p. 69.

26 In a recent survey conducted for the *ABA Journal* and the ABA's Division for Public Education, nearly 30 percent of the survey respondents said they lacked confidence that a jury would reach a fair verdict in a criminal matter. See "In the Shoes of the Accused," *ABA Journal,* June 1995, at p. 32.

27 Abramson, at pp. 102-104.

28 Laurie P. Cohen, "Southern Exposure: Lawyer Gets Investors, GE, Prudential in Poor Border Town," *Wall Street Journal,* November 30, 1994, at p. A-1.

29 Claudia Wilson Frost, Matthew P. Eastus, and David Hricik, "Discovery Abuse and Reform," *State Civil Justice Reform* (Washington, DC: National Legal Center for the Public Interest, 1994), at p. 115.

30 Federal Bar Association of the Western District of Washington, "Professionalism Task Force Interim Report," December 1994, at pp. 1-6.

31 Presentation of Cynthia Munger of Altman Weil Pensa, Inc., at Tulane Law Institute, March 31, 1995.

32 See Dissent to Supreme Court Order of April 29, 1980, in *Federal Civil Judicial Procedure and Rules* (Saint Paul: West Publishing Company, 1994), at p. 16.

33 Notes of Advisory Committee, 1983 Amendment to Rule 26.

34 Walter Olson, *The Litigation Explosion* (New York: Dutton, 1991), at pp. 117-118.

35 "A Litigator's Lament," at p. 80. Italics added.

36 Olson, at p. 299.

II. Civil justice for the new millennium

Chapter Three
Flawed Debates and
Partial Fixes

In 1776, Yale University President Timothy Dwight addressed a group of future lawyers. He admonished them to avoid:

"That meannness, that infernal knavery, which multiplies endless litigations, which retards the operation of justice, which from court to court, upon the most trifling pretences, postpones trial to glean the last emptyings of a client's pocket, for unjust fees of everlasting attendance, which artfully twists the meaning of law to the side we espouse, which seizes unwarrantable advantages from the prepossessions, ignorance, interests, and prejudices of a jury . . ."[1]

A casual reader, or someone committed to the status quo, might dismiss this centuries-old sermon with "So what? Some problems are eternal." Indeed, some are. But when Rev. Dwight addressed those students, the law was on the cusp of a profound reformation, intended to fix a system that made such abuses possible and profitable, and to craft a system that would work in the Industrial Age. To a remarkable extent, those reforms succeeded. And now it is time to do it again: time for a movement that, once more, will fix a system in which process has come to dominate substance and suborn justice . . . and also to craft a system to meet the needs of a new century and a rapidly changing society.

The alternative is to suffer under an ever more unjust, inequitable, and economically and socially destructive anachronism, and risk the consequences of that system's slow collapse.

Fortunately, a serious reform movement is, if not yet fully underway, certainly beginning to take shape. Civil justice reform has been one of the hotter legal topics of the 1990s. Indeed, it sometimes seems that two cottage industries have arisen – one dedicated to the manufacture of critiques and proposals, the other devoted to tearing them down and tearing them up.

Two significant pieces of federal legislation have already made it onto the statute books. One, the General Aviation Revitalization Act of 1994, which established reasonable product liability limits on single-engine piston aircraft, has started the resurrection of an industry virtually destroyed by predatory lawsuits. This act was unusual, in that it was fostered by an alliance of manufacturers, organized labor, and the Aircraft Owners and Pilots Association, perhaps the first time in history that a group of consumers (and potential plaintiffs) demanded limits on their right to sue. It was also unusual in that Cessna, a major manufacturer of small aircraft that had closed its single-engine piston line, promised to get back into the business if the act was passed. The company kept its word; several thousand new jobs have ensued. In 1996, general aviation manufacturers delivered the highest number of aircraft since 1990 and experienced their best gross revenue year in history. The General Aviation Manufacturers Association estimates that, because of the new limits (which ban product liability on parts after eighteen years), between 1997 and 2000 more new models will be introduced than in the whole preceding decade.[2]

The other significant federal statutory change was the Private Securities Litigation Reform Act of 1995, passed over President Clinton's veto, which adopted a variety of measures to decrease the number of frivolous securities fraud lawsuits and to limit liability. Among the significant changes: allowing for proportionate instead of joint-and-several liability (assessing damages among groups of defendants based upon the percentage of actual harm done, not the ability to pay). Also significant: protection from fraud suits when business predictions don't work out, but were made in good faith and accompanied by appropriate cautions against excessive investor reliance.[3]

Finally, the states have started passing partial reform legislation for their own systems. According to the American Tort Reform Association (ATRA), 45 states have enacted some sort of legislation since 1985.[4] In 1995, more than 70 reform bills, most dealing with limiting liability or capping or abolishing punitive damages, received consideration in various state legislatures. A survey by the Court Statistics Project of the National Center for State Courts found that such measures generally led to reductions in the number of filings. In two states that adopted significant tort reform measures, California and Colorado, filings fell over 20 percent in two years.[5] Once again, the states are acting as the "laboratories of democracy" so valued during the Progressive Era, conducting experiments and offering models that may have national significance in the coming years.

These partial fixes and hopeful experiments notwithstanding, legal reform still remains more a hot topic than an effective movement. There are two reasons for this. One is that the reform debate, like so many volatile topics, has been poorly structured, artificially and wrongly polarized, and strident. Popular understanding of the deeper issues has been rendered difficult. The second reason is that much of the reform effort either focuses on single issues or offers wide-ranging critiques, but shies away from presenting equivalent remedies.

This chapter sketches the present debate, then assesses various partial reform proposals and alternatives. Most of these proposals have value. Many are included in my own CORE Court reform plan. However, these proposals are interim measures at best, necessary but not sufficient for fundamental change. To repeat:

The present problem is a system run amok. But the deeper challenge is crafting a system that will meet the needs of a diverse, Information Age, 21st century society – a society that, increasingly, will conduct its business in cyberspace.

THE PRESENT DEBATE

There are two great conceptual obstacles to serious civil justice reform. The first is that the entire debate has been miscast as "Business" (sometimes "Big Business") versus "Consumers." In reality, the Business camp may be more representative of the people, and more responsive to the common good, than the Consumer activists.

To explain:

In the present, dubiously structured debate, the Business camp has been represented primarily by the industries most adversely affected by predatory and excessive litigation. These include public companies fearful of securities or other class-action claims and manufacturers concerned about product liability. Yet this camp also includes the professions: doctors fearful of medical malpractice claims and accountants worried about joint-and-several liability in securities cases. But membership in this camp does not end there. Rightfully, the Business camp *should* include everybody who knows that, someday, something might happen to involve him or her in a long, costly, and possibly unwarranted lawsuit. According to a national survey done for the American Tort Reform Association (ATRA), fully two-thirds of the respondents agreed with the statement: "I am afraid that one day I, or someone in my family, will be the victim of a frivolous lawsuit."[6]

There is a certain irony here. Consumer activists often proclaim that, since we are all consumers, they speak for everybody and, in any event, we're all potential plaintiffs. But the Reform camp – the proper name of the Business camp – should make a similar claim. We're also all potential defendants.

Obviously, some of the calls for reform reflect self-interest. Firms and individuals want to protect themselves. Demands for product liability reform and other limits can be self-serving. But self-interest does not automatically equate to venality or dishonesty. Nor does it invalidate the larger issues. Nor does it reflect the fact that many companies and individuals are already protecting themselves by not doing things they would otherwise do, for fear of lawsuits: cutting services, closing facilities, not developing new products. And, of course, many companies are not doing things they might have done because the necessary money went to pay for lawsuits, judgments, and insurance. How do we measure the good things that never happen, the potential markets and jobs lost to foreign competitors? How do we tally all the community volunteers who aren't there because of fear of lawsuits? The obvious costs are enormous, the hidden costs probably far greater.

In economics, the concept of "opportunity cost" says that the true cost of anything must be defined by the alternatives foregone. What has been the opportunity cost of unrestrained litigation? And what will be the opportunity cost if the system continues unchanged?

Arrayed against the Reform group is the "Consumer" camp, which might be called the Anti-Reform camp because it seeks to preserve the legal status quo. This Anti-Reform camp supports and defends the extensive and intensive use of lawsuits as a means of enforcing corporate honesty: the "invisible fist" theory. According to this notion, lawsuits and threat of lawsuits provide a discipline over and above that enforced by the market and governmental regulation. The theory is that fear of lawsuits, perhaps even more than fear of criminal prosecution, keeps individuals and businesses from breaking the law or from turning out inferior or dangerous products and shoddy services.

But in today's environment, the "invisible fist" can have a reverse effect. Fear of ruinous lawsuits may actually keep people from doing their best. This was certainly true in the general aviation industry before reform. Manufacturers declined to improve their aircraft because improvements could be construed as admission of previous defects, exposing the company to further liability risks. As a result, today, a single-engine aircraft costs considerably more than it should and lags two to three generations behind in propulsion and navigation technologies.

Is it irony or absurdity when the fear of lawsuits keeps people from admitting and correcting their mistakes, and when such honesty is deemed to make a company more vulnerable to the vagaries of the civil justice system? This "Don't Admit Anything" strategy has long been common in industries particularly susceptible to gargantuan lawsuits: aviation, autos, oil and chemicals, to name a few. But I wonder: Would a less confrontational, less winner-take-all legal environment have rendered these companies more willing to correct their mistakes before they led to greater damage and/or disaster?

In addition to the consumer groups, the real champions of the Anti-Reform effort are those with much at stake financially: the plaintiffs' lawyers themselves, organized nationally as the American Trial Lawyers Association. ATLA is highly visible, well-funded, well-connected, and generous to those politicians who support its agenda. According to the most recent figures available from the Federal Election Commission website (http://www.fec.gov/finance/pacdisye.html), in 1996 the group gave nearly $5.1 million to various candidates of both parties in the presidential and congressional races.

In the present debate, both the Reform and Anti-Reform camps use the same types of evidence and argument to support their positions. First, each draws upon actual cases, especially of the "horror story" variety. Reform proponents cite cases in which plaintiffs received damages clearly excessive to the harm suffered, or in which judges turned a blind eye to highly abusive discovery practices, or in which defendants who were minimally at fault compared to others in the same case had to pay a disproportionate share simply because they had deeper pockets. Anti-Reform activists cite cases in which egregious acts were punished by awards that barely compensated the plaintiffs. They also point to cases in which a plaintiff's persistence in pre-trial discovery finally located a "smoking gun" that established the defendant's unsavory nature and nailed his or her culpability.

In addition to arguments over opportunity costs and invisible fists, the two camps raise several other arguments. The Reform camp notes that, in the end, the consumer actually bears the cost of this "protection." When a business pays a big damage award, prices for its products and services inevitably rise. This means, among other things, that American products do less well against foreign competition, at home and in the global economy.

The Anti-Reform camp also points out that because government cannot muster sufficient resources to enforce every law all the time (arguably a fortuitous defect, given all the laws on the books), we need a legal system that encourages plaintiffs to function as "private prosecuting attorneys." They also stress the importance of the right to sue, arguing that reform would limit the average citizen's access to justice through the courts. They assert that, while some defendants have been hit with improper and excessive damage awards, on balance this is preferable to leaving the injured without remedy, especially since defendants earn money from the business activities that harm plaintiffs.

One need not be an especially Good Samaritan to begin to pity the poor legislators who have to sort out these arguments, and the interests and rationales behind them. Of course, sorting out may not be necessary since, for the most part, these arguments and examples tend to cancel out. As the *Wall Street Journal* put it: "The debate over curbing personal injury and other lawsuits has degenerated into a duel of self-serving polls, studies, and 'horror stories' that aren't always what they seem."[7]

In other words, the reform debate has taken on the form of most other contemporary disputations: ill-framed and hyperbolically argued, with both sides shouting "You, too" and "What about?" Meanwhile the system chugs on, with its faults and deficiencies ever more apparent.

But even if it were possible to get beyond the rhetoric, an additional problem would be the current focus on partial fixes. While the American people as a whole grow increasingly skeptical, most of those who study legal reform still argue that the system is basically OK, with only a few adjustments needed. Just reform discovery procedures a bit, limit punitive damages a little, rein in contingent fees, whatever. Then all will be well, and the game can go on.

But the game can't go on. The proposals considered below are *necessary but insufficient.* They have considerable merit as partial correctives and palliatives and should be enacted and/ or implemented. But none of them, nor even all of them together, can solve the underlying problem of the increasing mismatch between this society's 21st century legal needs and its Industrial Age system.

PARTIAL FIXES: THE PARTIES

These proposals address many aspects of the current system: ethical standards, procedural reforms, the roles of judge and jury, the nature and extent of damage awards, and the uses of Alternative Dispute Resolution. But it's important to remember that the adversary system consists not merely of a thousand different human bits and procedural pieces. It's made of three interacting major components: the parties involved (clients and attorneys), the decision-makers involved (judges and juries), and the rules and procedures involved. So we'll consider some of the individual proposals as they fit within the general categories.

The Clients

I cannot state it too often. The client must remember that he or she is in charge; that it's the client's case, not the attorney's; and that the attorney has a fiduciary responsibility to place the client's interests first. At its highest, civil law aspires to justice, the proper redress of grievance. But it also serves as a workaday means of dispute and grievance resolution, and sometimes resolving the dispute matters more than exacting that last ounce of retribution for self or "society." This is certainly true for parties who have to deal with each other afterwards: divorcing parents, franchisor and franchisee, even folks who can expect to see each other in church next Sunday. Not so many decades ago, lawyers were taught and expected to keep their clients out of court whenever possible. Litigation was the last resort. Today, more and more businesses (and perhaps more and more lawyers) are again recognizing the value of this principled reluctance to head for court at each and every opportunity. Therefore, the first reform proposal we consider is, in many ways, the most radical . . . and the most common-sensical.

If you can reasonably do so, solve your problem without a lawsuit.

Alternative Dispute Resolution (ADR)

It is certainly revealing that one of the most promising "reforms," ADR, is taking place more or less outside the civil justice system. ADR encompasses a wide variety of dispute resolution procedures, most notably arbitration and mediation. The 1990s have seen the ADR industry grow substantially. More and more companies are demanding ADR clauses in contracts; the federal government, with the support of the American Bar Association (ABA), is increasing its use.[8] Some localities have even established ADR facilities within the court system.

One example: In 1995, several hundred potential litigants in Thurston County, Washington, participated in a week-long courthouse ADR experiment. Over half the cases presented for ADR were resolved. According to a report in the *Washington State Bar News*, the experiment demonstrated that "Court-annexed ADR rewards courts with cost-savings and civil backlog reductions, and benefits litigants by resolving cases sooner and for less money. Moreover, court-annexation ensures that ADR services are broadly accessible, and demonstrates the legal community's commitment to providing the best ways to solve legal problems."[9]

In another experiment, the "Early Assessment Program" conducted by the U.S. District Court for the Western District of Missouri (one of five pilot projects mandated by the 1990 Civil Justice Reform Act), over half the 1,321 participating attorneys found court-annexed ADR "very helpful" in reducing costs. Over three-quarters believed the benefits of the process outweighed the costs.[10]

These happy results notwithstanding, for the foreseeable future the largest ADR providers will continue to be non-profit corporations such as the American Arbitration Association (AAA) and the CPR Institute for Dispute Resolution, as well as for-profit entities such as Judicial Arbitration & Mediation Services and U.S. Arbitration and Mediation. These companies offer a variety of fee-based services, from counseling and contract documentation to providing private judges, arbitrators, and mediators. Also, an unknown but apparently increasing number of law firms and attorneys now offer ADR as a formal or informal adjunct to their standard services.

ADR is an "alternative" precisely because it has developed outside the public litigation system. One commentator has referred to ADR as "the emergence of a [free] market in dispute resolution which is challenging the traditional state-owned monopoly in dispute resolution."[11] As previously noted, there are various forms of ADR, but by far the most common are arbitration (letting a chosen third party resolve the dispute) and mediation (letting a chosen third party bring the disputants to agreement).

Arbitration has been available to American litigants for nearly a century; the AAA is over seventy years old. In many ways, arbitration is a "skinnied-down" version of litigation. The parties agree to abide by certain rules, covering everything from the arbitration site to the types of discovery applicable to the proceedings. In lieu of judge and jury, the parties agree that one or more neutral arbitrators will resolve the dispute after hearing the evidence. Although the arbitrators are neutral, they typically have special expertise in the subject under dispute. The arbitration rules can be as simple or complex as the parties and the arbitrators desire. In most cases, the parties agree that the decision will be binding. No appeals to the court system are allowed.

Arbitration also has become increasingly popular as a means of settling disputes between corporations and consumers of their goods and services. Predictably, consumer advocates have opposed this trend. "Americans are giving up their right to sue," proclaimed an article in the *New York Times*. "To sue their banks over credit card and account disputes. To sue their real estate agents over deals gone awry. To sue their mortgage companies over false advertising. To sue their doctors for malpractice or their health plans over coverage. Even to sue a computer maker over a defective machine."[12] Consumer advocates contend that people are losing this right without even knowing it, since arbitration clauses are often buried in the fine print, and that private arbitration deprives the public of information about corporate malfeasance that would come out in public trials. Consumer advocates also believe that the odds favor companies who go through the process repeatedly against one-time customer complainants. Yet the article reports that some companies experience the opposite effect. Complainants seem to win more often in arbitration than in litigation, although the awards tend to be smaller.

But the most explosive growth in ADR recently has come from mediation, which differs dramatically from arbitration. In mediation, the parties agree to a mediator (or sometimes a panel of mediators) to help them negotiate a resolution. The mediator is generally referred to as a "neutral." The mediator's job is to confer with the parties, separately and together, in order to reach a mutually satisfactory resolution. While mediation is not binding – the parties may still end up in court – most mediations do resolve the dispute at hand, usually at substantial savings in time and money over full litigation.[13]

Business has grown enthusiastic about ADR. In 1993, Deloitte & Touche, a major accounting firm, surveyed nearly 250 large corporate ADR users and concluded that "satisfaction with ADR is generally high."[14] The survey also indicated that participants intended to expand their use of ADR in the future. A 1992 *Business Week* survey of 400 large companies found that over 97 percent of respondents favored "much greater use" of ADR and its methods."[15] And in 1994, the CPR Institute for Dispute Resolution reported that 850 corporations, on their own behalf and for their 2,800 subsidiaries, had signed the "CPR Corporate Policy Statement on Alternatives to Litigation," which committed them to explore ADR before resorting to litigation.[16]

Businesses have flocked to ADR for several reasons. The most common is that ADR tends to be faster and cheaper than litigation. For example, the CPR Institute reported that between 1990 and 1993 its personnel helped resolve disputes involving nearly $7 billion in claims, and that ADR had saved the parties an estimated $187 million in legal costs. Savings averaged about $425,000 per party involved.[17]

Another reason businesses like ADR is that it often allows the disputants to reach agreement without the hostility associated with court litigation. This is especially valuable in an age when many companies have to form alliances — and establish reputations as good allies — in order to compete in the globalizing market. As the general counsel of Pizza Hut explained when asked why his company preferred to mediate disputes with franchisees: "If you have a situation where you're litigating with your partner it tends to dissolve the relationship."[18]

International ADR is also becoming more common. As cross-national relationships grow, so do cross-national frictions and disputes. It is far easier to maintain these potentially volatile relationships when disputes can be settled relatively quickly and amicably through a mechanism that takes account of cultural differences. Also, ADR can be structured to provide genuinely neutral turf. A dispute between an American and a Japanese company, for example, could be resolved by a panel of mediators from both countries, or from neither. Transnational litigation within a national court system almost inevitably leaves one of the parties disadvantaged, or at least feeling that way.

The attitude of the legal profession toward ADR, as mentioned above, has grown more positive in recent years. However, it remains ambivalent. Given that cost savings come out of litigators' potential incomes, it is not surprising that some would prefer not to endorse the ADR concept, or even let their clients know about its popularity and availability. Other attorneys have started touting their own skills as arbitrators or mediators, and their willingness to act as "counselors" to clients during ADR processes.[19] Some of this new acceptance represents, no doubt, an attempt to recapture lost real and potential income. But much of it also suggests surrender to the inevitable.

And inevitable it may be. Some courts, pressured by over-crowded dockets, now routinely recommend or require litigants to participate in non-binding ADR during the pre-trial period. And, as mentioned, even the federal government has grown more accepting. In February 1996, President Clinton signed an Executive Order directing agencies to make greater use of ADR. Since then, the Justice Department has ruled that federal agencies may enter binding arbitration if they wish, ending a long-standing ban.[20]

Finally, according to the 1992 *ABA Blueprint for Improving the Civil Justice System,* more than 94 percent of law schools now offer dispute resolution courses and more than half the nation's state and local bar associations have dispute resolution committees.[21]

Still, ADR has raised several concerns. One is that private ADR organizations can, or could, entice significant numbers of good jurists away from the public court system. Today, experienced judges can often receive higher salaries from private ADR entities than they can earn as civil servants. This concern has grown so serious that, in some states, sitting judges are now permitted to "moonlight" for private ADR providers. In Connecticut, for example, judges can now work for a mediation company whose founder had grown concerned that "justice was slipping out of the public court system, and out of the hands of judges."[22] The irony is apt: the private sector hiring judges because they can no longer function properly in public courtrooms.

A second concern pertains to the law itself. As more cases are resolved through ADR, the common law may suffer. This may be especially true if pivotal cases in emerging high-tech industries end up in ADR. Since the common law is governed by *stare decisis,* by precedents established in earlier cases, there is a real danger that ADR will drain off important precedent-setting cases. Law is always being refined. But in ADR, decisions are made with no binding reference to legal precedent and are often confidential. If the common law grows "stale," or if it cannot keep up with new activities and situations, everyone will suffer.

A third problem involves the use of non-lawyer ADR personnel. Typically, these people emphasize that they do not and may not give "legal advice." But the line between discussing legal matters – and these disputes involve, in the vast majority of cases, legal matters – and "giving advice" is a fine one. This may not matter so much when the disputants are corporations and have their own staff and outside attorneys. But in areas such as family law, where the disputes can be uniquely intense and one or both parties may be unadvised and poor, the results can be devastating. Linda M. Roubik, a Seattle family law attorney, believes that ADR should have little place in divorce financial settlements, especially when there is a power imbalance between husband and wife. According to Roubik: "People coming into this [ADR] forum, especially unrepresented people, want information. To whatever extent a mediator makes comments regarding rights and responsibilities, or the general state of the law, he or she is giving legal advice."[23]

On the other hand, legal advice can be crucial by its absence. For example, a mediator may recommend child support payments well below what a judge has the power to order. A mother of modest means who is probably in a state of extreme emotional turmoil may not know this. Probably, a father in possession of this information will not volunteer it. And a mediator, whose purpose is resolution, may strive for resolution even when it may not be in one parent's best interest.

On balance, though, ADR's virtues outweigh its defects and dangers – if only because ADR has not yet become sufficiently common for those defects and dangers to start causing widespread harm. Its advantages lie in its flexibility with respect to rules, its emphasis on settlement without rancor, and its relative cheapness.

However, ADR can never replace, and should not be expected to replace, institutional justice. It should never evolve into a "parallel system of justice." And, in its present form, it will always be a "partial fix," lightening the load on a collapsing system and offering convenient alternatives without addressing larger problems.

The Lawyers

In the last chapter, I suggested that something has gone seriously wrong with lawyering, and with the delicate balances involved in the practice of law. The ethical attorney must place his or her client's interests first. Providing "zealous representation" is just as much a moral imperative as not defrauding or neglecting the client's interests. But an attorney is also an "officer of the court," exercising certain powers, such as subpoena, on behalf of the court and society. Indeed, in no other democratic country do private citizens —and attorneys are private citizens— enjoy such prerogatives. Finally, every attorney has an ethical obligation to conduct himself or herself in a manner that contributes to the smooth functioning of, and increases respect for, the law and the system that administers it.

In recent years, however, the practice of law has been coarsened. Although this coarsening is not unique to the profession, it is particularly abhorrent in the practice of law, because of the law's custodial nature. If one partial fix is simply to resolve more disputes without lawsuits, another is for the legal profession to recover and enforce a higher sense of what it means to be and act like a professional, and indeed a more postive member of society. Excess, whether of aggressiveness or abrasiveness, should not be the norm, or be perceived as the norm.

The ABA has recognized and tried to counter this negative trend in lawyering. In addition, various other legal groups have tried to address the growing incidence of discourteous, "if it's legal it's OK," and outright "I can get away with it" behavior by lawyers intent upon winning at all costs. Many state bar associations, for example, now require continuing legal education in professional ethics for their members.

The King County (Washington) Bar Association has published a pamphlet with ten "Guidelines of Professional Courtesy." They are worth citing in full, not because of their new or strikingly original demands, but precisely because of their prosaic nature.

1. A lawyer should always treat others with courtesy and respect.
2. A lawyer should honor promises and commitments.
3. A lawyer should never knowingly deceive another.
4. A lawyer should make reasonable efforts to schedule matters with other counsel by agreement.
5. A lawyer should be timely in responding to other lawyers and considerate of their time.
6. A lawyer should not seek sanctions against opposing counsel for mere tactical advantage.
7. A lawyer should not make unfounded accusations of unethical conduct about opposing counsel.
8. A lawyer should be punctual.
9. A lawyer should seek informal agreement on procedural and preliminary matters.
10. A lawyer should not engage in invidious discrimination.

This pamphlet, which was distributed to all members of the bar association, states that the guidelines are not mandatory but are "intended to guide [lawyers'] individual ethics."

And thus another partial fix: the restoration of high standards of professional conduct and civility. It would be welcome indeed. But it would still be partial.

PARTIAL FIXES: THE DECISION-MAKERS

The second major component of the modern adversary system, the neutral and passive decision-makers of the bench and the jury box, certainly inspire more general respect than the lawyers and the rules. Perhaps no part of the system is more sacrosanct in theory (and even in popular sensibility) than the jury of lay peers. And certainly the office of judge still commands considerable popular respect. A special scorn is reserved for corrupt or incompetent judges. But neither institution emerged without a long and often turbulent history.

Today, the next evolution is due. When any institution no longer upholds the principles it was established to uphold, it's time either to abandon the principles or change the institution. To abandon the principles of neutrality, objectivity and rationality is unthinkable. The institution must be changed.

In fact, there is no shortage of recommendations and proposals for improving the functioning of the judge and jury. There are also a number of worthy experiments underway, including making jury duty more palatable for jurors. They are explored here as good measures in their own right, but again, as only partial solutions unless they're part of a more comprehensive reform.

The Jury

Eight hundred or so years ago, English juries were royal instruments, convened at the king's command. But the legitimacy of the jury derived at least as much from its own composition as from royal fiat. Jurors were local notables, with their own reputations and resources. They sat in judgment on defendants of whom they usually had personal knowledge, and sometimes personal prejudice. But the reverse is equally important. The litigants and the general community also knew the jurors. The jurors were men of special position whose powers and position depended, to an extent not often recognized today, on their own conduct and reputation.

Half a millennium later, three revolutionary legal concepts had emerged. One was that a jury ought to be composed of "legal peers," not social elites or royal agents. Another was that jurors should either have no personal knowledge of the events and people before them, or else disregard that knowledge. A final concept was that the jury should be passive prior to the start of its formal deliberations.

Today, these notions have been either distorted or rendered obsolete. Jurors are now often viewed as "representative" of social, ethnic, racial, and economic groups – which can strain the idea of "legal peer" juries chosen from the general population. Jurors are now too often chosen and valued, not for their knowledge or their impartiality, but for their ignorance and their prejudices. And finally, the requirement for passivity, which bars the jury from seeking the kinds of information it needs to do its decision-making job, exacerbates the effects of ignorance and prejudice.

In a civil justice system dedicated to fairness and rationality, ignorance and prejudice do not have a place. They didn't during the Industrial Age. They certainly don't in the emerging Information Age, where even "routine" cases can exhibit extreme complexity.

In short, without decision-makers who possess or can acquire adequate information, 21st century civil justice cannot and will not work.

In this area, even the most ardent defenders of the present system admit that some partial fixes might be useful. One relates to jury size, and changes are already underway. The trend at the state and local levels is clearly away from the traditional twelve-person jury. In the 1970s, the Supreme Court ruled twice that this size is not constitutionally mandated in civil cases. In 1991, the Judicial Conference, the judiciary's policy-making arm, changed Rule 48 of the Federal Rules of Civil Procedure to authorize smaller juries. By 1993, 39 states and the District of Columbia had instituted smaller juries for at least some kinds of civil cases. Another trend: moving away from the requirement for unanimous verdicts. Fewer than twenty states and the District of Columbia still require unanimous verdicts in all subjects.[24]

Still, whatever the jury's size, the problems of ignorance and evidence that is too difficult to understand remain. There are currently a number of proposals and experiments underway to help lay jurors master the legal and evidentiary material before them. A 1992 Brookings Institution/ABA joint study proposed greater jury activity and better comprehension aids. In the first category, activity, the study urged that jurors be allowed to submit written questions to witnesses through the judge. The study, however, stopped short of calling for a juror's right to request witnesses or other material. The study also recommended that jurors be given the right to discuss the case with each other prior to final deliberation. The study did not, however, call for any direct interaction between the jury and judge, or between the jury and the parties' attorneys.

In the second category – comprehension aids – the study offered a range of reforms:

- Jurors should be allowed to take notes.
- Jurors should be given exhibit notebooks.
- Computers should provide "on-line" records of testimony during deliberations.
- Modern audio-visual aids should be employed.
- Attorneys should be allowed to make "mini-summaries" throughout the trial.[25]

It is difficult to disagree with any of these common-sense proposals or to find evidence of courtroom experiments where they did not bring about some improvement. But it remains doubtful whether even the most advanced multimedia displays or an endless right to submit questions will reliably provide the minimal knowledge and understanding necessary to evaluate fairly the highly technical evidence and issues that underlie many Information Age disputes.

In sum, the jury is indeed a vital part of the American justice system. The principles it reifies must be retained. But that does not make the jury, or a jury of a particular size, the correct instrument in all cases. Nor can the requirement for impartiality any longer be miscast as ignorance, or the requirement for social diversity be used as a guise for prejudice.

The Judge

Of all the components of the present adversary system, the role of the judge might seem the least impaired. However, it is clear that many members of the judiciary understand, at least as well as do attorneys, that the system is in chronic crisis. Consider the results of a survey.

In 1992, the Federal Judicial Center, the research and planning agency of the federal judicial system, surveyed the federal judiciary on the state of their institution. Over 80 percent of those approached, judges, magistrates, and staff, took the time to answer an in-depth questionnaire. The results are remarkable.

- 82.5 percent of responding federal circuit court judges said that increasingly complex caseloads are a problem. Specialized court judges (Bankruptcy, Court of Claims, International Trade Court) rated the problem as more severe than circuit or district court judges.
- 34.7 percent of responding federal judges believed that expert jury panels should be used in certain types of cases.
- 68 percent of federal district court judges supported the increased use of court-appointed experts.
- 60.1 percent of federal circuit court judges supported in-

creased use of ADR.

- 66.1 percent of federal district court judges disagreed with the proposition that civil cases should be resolved only through traditional litigation.

The 110 page document is filled with similar findings.[26]

Beyond such suggestions, there are other areas in which the judiciary, especially at the trial level, is now being exhorted toward change.

The first exhortation is to "take back the courtroom" – and especially to rein in attorneys whose tactics become too aggressive or abrasive, or clearly questionable. It is understandable that trial judges, in their desire to avoid having their decisions reversed on appeal, would want to give contending counsel every opportunity to present their cases. But standards of decorum and procedure must be enforced. And some commentators have noted that a more rigorous enforcement would provide incentives toward greater civility and professionalism on the part of the bar in general.

In addition to enforcing standards of decorum and conduct, judges are being advised to draw upon an array of management techniques. The ABA's Ad Hoc Committee on Civil Justice Improvements has recommended a number of new procedures to facilitate settlements early in the life of a case and has identified a number of management techniques, such as convening settlement conferences early in the pre-trial phase of a lawsuit. The Committee has acknowledged that these recommendations are "modest," due to the need to achieve consensus.[27]

Unfortunately, given the present state of the system, "modest" recommendations will usually have less than modest results. A recent study by the RAND Institute for Civil Justice, which raised a number of judicial eyebrows, makes this point dramatically. The Civil Justice Reform Act of 1990 required each federal district to develop a civil case management plan using various techniques, including ADR and limits on discovery, to facilitate early settlement of cases. But according to the 1997 RAND study, these management packages "failed to have much effect on either time delays or costs in the federal courts."[28] In fact, the study found that early and active management of cases by judges "reduced time to disposition by about 1.5 months but resulted in [government] costs per litigation that were $3,000 higher. And lawyer work hours were found to be 35 hours longer than in other cases."[29]

Clearly, each part of the management package, especially ADR and discovery limits, has value. Few deny that they should be available. But it is also becoming clear that modest and conventional reform packages and improved managerial techniques are not sufficient to redeem the system.

Judges also are being exhorted to use the powers now evolving, via Supreme Court decisions and other developments, to curb some of the existing abuses. At the moment, there is evidence of a changing sensibility among some judges, a kind of "I'm not going to put up with it anymore" attitude toward two major areas of abuse – class-action suits and excessive damage awards. Some of this has taken the form of cracking down on outrageous legal fees and questionable settlements. In 1996, Russell Lloyd, a state judge in Texas, cut a Houston attorney's fees and expenses from $108.8 million to $43.5 million in a class-action involving faulty polybutylene plumbing. Judge Lloyd cited the judge's role as "guardian" of the system.[30] In another case, *Brand Name Prescription Drugs Antitrust Litigation*, involving a class-action by several thousand pharmacists against pharmaceutical firms for alleged price-fixing, plaintiffs' lawyers settled with 15 of 22 defendants for $408 million. Under the arrangements, a consortium of law firms would split $122 million, while the pharmacists got about $10,000 each . . . from a settlement that never addressed the central issue of price-fixing. The pharmacists went to court. U.S. District Judge Charles P. Kocoras in Chicago threw the settlement out.[31]

If an increasing number of judges at the trial level are saying, "Enough is enough," the Supreme Court has also said it in the matter of punitive damages. Or, more aptly, "Enough can be too much." In 1996, in *BMW v. Gore*, the Court ruled that punitive damages can be set so high as to be an unconstitutional violation of due process.[32] This was the case that gave an Alabama physician $4 million in settlement for a defective paint job on his BMW. Still, the Court declined to impose clear caps on punitives, noting only that lower courts should consider the following factors: the reprehensibility of the defendant's conduct, the ratio between punitive and compensatory damages, and the difference between the punitive award and the amount that could be imposed for comparable misconduct via civil or criminal sanctions.[33] This is a common-sense approach which, if properly applied, could lessen the outrages. It is also worth noting that, since 1986, 31 states have enacted legislation prohibiting, limiting, or otherwise regulating punitive damages.

PARTIAL FIXES: THE PROCEDURES

Clients have lost control of their cases to their lawyers. Judge and jury can no longer function as envisioned or required. And the third element of the adversary system – the rules governing how the litigants, their lawyers, and the decision-makers act and interact – have been distorted in effect. So it's not surprising that many of the proposals for legislative tort reform have addressed these rules. The Private Securities Litigation Reform Act of 1995, for example, covers procedural issues such as which facts must be known to a lawyer before a securities fraud claim can even be filed in federal court, and when discovery in a securities fraud case can be initiated. It's also not surprising, given the contemporary litigators' use of the rules as weapons, that the trial lawyers have been fiercely resistant to changes that would lessen the power of those weapons.

Most of the recent proposals for changes in the rules focus on two key areas: those rules relating to the use of expert witnesses and those relating to discovery. As with the other reform efforts, the current proposals are worthwhile, but not sufficient to correct the deeper problems of the adversary system.

The Use of Expert Witnesses

In theory, the adversary system requires that the decision-makers know only what is properly presented to them. The parties-in-interest and their counsel provide the witnesses, exhibits, and documentation. But for matters involving scientific, technical, and other specialized information, the Rules of Evidence also provide that expert witnesses may be used to introduce and express opinions on the evidence. In the vast majority of cases, these experts are brought into the litigation by the opposing parties.

And therein lies the problem. An entire industry of hired-gun experts, whose testimony is more-or-less expert but also clearly partisan, has arisen. Some of these people earn all or much of their income, not by practicing in their own fields as doctors, scientists, engineers, or technicians, but through employment as experts in various lawsuits. These people are hired precisely because their testimony regarding the scientific or technical evidence at hand will be helpful to the hiring party. Their job is to convince the jury that their analysis and interpretation of some key evidence is correct – or, at least, correct enough to cancel out the opinions of the opposing party's experts.

This provides yet another irony (or absurdity) in today's civil justice system. Experts are brought into a case precisely because the scientific or technical evidence at hand is too difficult for the judge and jury to understand without specialized help. But, as usually happens when the parties each provide their own experts, the hired guns disagree on the proper meaning and interpretation of the evidence. And often the decision-makers – especially the jury – are rendered more bewildered than before. If the experts cannot agree, how can lay people with no experience in the field even begin to assess the validity of the evidence in question? So the decision-makers are left once again with little substance and lots of raw adversarial process, which the opposing lawyers then try to exploit for their own purposes.

This creation of "bafflement via conflicting expertise" corrupts the entire decision-making process. It's not just the way in which the experts often cancel out. The problem is also the way in which some experts, and some fields of expertise, triumph over others by exploiting juror sensibilities unrelated to the case at hand.

Further, the ability of experts to cancel each other out is due to more than each side's desire to neutralize the other's hired guns. In most fields, there are legitimate and often major differences over certain issues. Attorneys are able to exploit these differences. As Joe Jamail, a highly successful tort attorney, once put it: "I don't need all the science to be on my side. Any good trial lawyer knows that if you've got one credible expert or scientific study then you can let the jury decide."[34]

In addition to credible studies and experts, there is also an enormous tonnage of "junk science" out there. The term "junk science" can mean simply sloppy, error-laden research and unwarranted conclusions. It can also refer to theories created to advance particular political, cultural, or social agendas. And it can mean (this is an especially delicate area) theories that are not – or not yet – widely accepted as accurate within the relevant scientific or technical communities, or endorsed by them as falling within the "realm of legitimate dispute."

I have already noted the increasing tendency of jurors to "vote their feelings," especially in complex or volatile cases. It now seems that jurors also "vote their feelings" when assessing expert witnesses. A small but growing body of research suggests that juror reactions to experts tend to be based as much upon personal factors as upon the evidence presented.[35]

Obviously, it always helps when the expert is a personable, attractive, credible sort. But other factors enter in. According to a review of the available jury-response literature in the *Jurimetrics Journal,* middle-class jurors tend to identify personally with experts yet treat their testimony with more skepticism than lower-class jurors, who give greater weight to credentials yet sometimes discount the testimony because they feel they're being "talked down to." Finally, the article notes that "When an expert's opinion is based upon a 'soft' science such as psychology, the standard for admissibility is often lower than when the opinion is based on a hard science such as chemistry."[36] In other words, the less precise an expert's field, the easier it is to be taken seriously.

The authors conclude that more research is needed to understand the dynamics of this set of contradictory conclusions. At the psychological level, this is no doubt true. But in terms of the workings of the adversary system, the effects are far more obvious. These effects are both corrupting and costly. As the President's Council on Competitiveness put it in their 1991 *Agenda for Civil Justice Reform:*

"An area of the law particularly ripe for reform is expert witness practice. The Federal Rules of Evidence, which govern most expert witness testimony, eliminated many of the common law restrictions on the use of expert witnesses. The resulting uncontrolled use of expert witnesses has led to longer trials, more expensive litigation, and a reduction in the quality of expert testimony in many cases."[37]

The legal profession has also recognized this problem. The ABA's *Blueprint for Improving the Civil Justice System* recommends that expert testimony be admissible only if it "is based on an established theory that is supported by a significant portion of experts in the relevant field."[38] This was, in fact, the standard mandated by the U.S. Court of Appeals for the District of Columbia in a 1923 case, *Frye v. United States*, and generally accepted at the state and federal levels for the next several decades.[39] The study also recommends closer scrutiny of professional credentials and banning contingent fees for experts. But the report does not fully endorse what may be the optimal solution: court-appointed experts or full-time staff experts.

However, the trend may be toward such experts. In the spring of 1996, several district judges in New York announced they would appoint a search team to establish a roster of neutral experts around the country to advise courts handling breast-implant cases.[40] Clearly, these judges were dissatisfied with both the quality and impartiality of the litigants' experts. In 1996, the Supreme Court decided, in *Markman v. Westview Instruments, Inc.*, to let judges, not juries, decide certain patent infringement claims.[41] The Court indicated that the complexity of these claims has grown beyond the lay person's ability to handle. To fulfill this role, judges would have to have their own sources of expertise. As one prominent patent law attorney summed the situation: "Some patented technology these days is incomprehensible even to those of us who do it for a living."[42] What is true for expert attorneys must also be true for judges.

Whatever the future may hold for court-appointed experts, there is clearly a trend toward correcting some of the more flagrant abuses involving expert testimony. In 1993, in *Daubert v. Merrell Dow Pharmaceuticals, Inc.*, the Supreme Court assigned judges greater powers as "gatekeepers" for admitting experts.[43] There is no current consensus on the extent of a judge's duty to keep dubious testimony out of court, or even what constitutes dubious testimony. But at least a few judges are willing to use the new empowerment. A recent example: The barring in several trials of questionable evidence purporting to show a link between cancer and electromagnetic fields generated by power transmission lines, calling a halt to a class-action movement that, potentially, could have turned half the people in America into plaintiffs.[44]

Discovery

For many observers of the adversary system's crisis, the greatest source of concern is attorney abuse of the discovery rules governing each side's right to seek information from the other. For some, the worry is that lawyers and their clients sometimes resist the rightful discovery requests of the opposing party. But for most, the primary concern is that Rule 26 of the Federal Rules of Procedure, allowing discovery of all potentially relevant information, is simply too broad, especially in the Information Age. Again, there is irony here. The greater the availability of information, the easier it becomes to pressure and intimidate the opposing party merely by asking for it. And, too often, the greater the information available, the more discovery leads to out-of-court settlement, not courtroom confrontation. *The quest for the facts becomes the means by which process overwhelms substance, and thereby undermines justice.*

In recent years, there have been numerous proposals, at both the federal and state court levels, to adopt more restricted discovery rules. These proposals involve, for example, limiting discovery requests to a set number at the beginning of the process, or requiring parties to hand over certain information without waiting for the other side to request it, or limiting the duration of the discovery process. Some of these proposals have been put forth by bar associations, some by courts, and some by proponents of legislative legal reform. Another idea, occasionally offered as a means of preventing discovery-as-extortion: "Loser pays." This has two variants. In one, the losing party picks up the winner's legal tab . . . certainly a powerful deterrent to launching frivolous yet expensive litigation. In another variant, the loser who has abused the rules pays the proportion of the winner's legal costs attributable to the abuse.

One current effort to reform discovery is particularly significant, not just because it attempts to reform the discovery process but because it introduces some new ideas about how courts should be organized. In 1994, the state of Delaware created a new court in response to the "litigation crisis." This new Business Court is available for the resolution of business disputes involving more than $1 million, provided all parties agree to have their disputes resolved under the procedures of the court. These procedures limit discovery's duration and scope. Discovery cannot continue past 180 days, and there are limits on the number of interrogatories and depositions available to each party. The procedures also require the trial to be completed in five days and preclude the award of punitive damages. There is no jury. The judge is experienced in business issues.

Delaware decided to establish this new court, with its streamlined procedures, after it surveyed corporate counsel throughout the country and found "a near unanimous result – traditional litigation is very unsatisfactory."[45] What makes this reform so appealing is that it focuses – actually, refocuses – the adversary process on the parties' presentation of evidence at trial, rather than on endless discovery and disputes over discovery.

This "toss the bath water, keep the baby" approach apparently has national appeal. Five other states – Illinois, New Jersey, New York, North Carolina, and Wisconsin – have similar courts. Ten more are considering adoption of some variant, including setting up court-annexed ADR. So far, results and satisfaction have been considerable, certainly when measured by time and expenses saved.[46] The Delaware Business Court, and no doubt the other courts already established and under consideration, have the potential to restore some validity to the notion that justice really is the goal of our civil justice system.

Summary

There is no shortage of good ideas out there, or good people to understand them. Nor is there any shortage of experiments, or good people to design and run them. I find the Delaware Business Court experiment the most resonant personally, but there are literally thousands of other reform attempts under consideration or underway, at all levels of government and the court system. These efforts should be supported. Many of them are included in my own CORE Court reform plan. Still, the present array of reform plans does not address the larger issue of how to bring the civil justice system into the Information Age. How do we craft an effective and equitable system for an ever-more transnational economy and ever-more-diverse society? Without such change, the good and valid principles underlying the adversary system will be lost.

We turn now to the task of crafting a civil justice system for the 21st century.

1 Quoted in Jethro K. Lieberman, *The Litigious Society* (New York: Basic Books, 1981), at p. 14.

2 Geoffrey A. Campbell, "Study: Business Booms after Tort Reform Enacted," *ABA Journal,* January 1996, at p. 28. See also General Aviation Manufacturers Association, "Annual Industry Review: 1997 Outlook and Agenda," GAMA, Washington, DC.

3 See John W. Avery, "Securities Litigation Reform," *The Business Lawyer,* February 1996, at pp. 335-378. Unfortunately, it now appears some of the benefits of this federal law may not be fully realized, for plaintiffs' lawyers have begun simply to bypass the federal courts and file their securities class-action claims in state courts. See Grundfest and Perino, "Securities Litigation Reform: The First Year's Experience," 1997, available on the Internet at http://securities.stanford.edu/report.

4 American Tort Reform Association, "Tort Reform Record," Washington, DC, 1996.

5 Martha Middleton, "A Changing Landscape," *ABA Journal,* August 1995, at p. 57.

6 Public Opinion Strategies, "Executive Summary: National Survey on Legal Liability Reform Issue" Conducted for American Tort Reform Association, Washington, D.C., 1995, at p. 6.

7 Richard B. Schmitt, "Truth Is the First Casualty of Tort-Reform Debate," *Wall Street Journal,* March 7, 1995, at p. B-1.

8 Rhonda McMillon, "Growing Acceptance for ADR," *ABA Journal,* May 1996, at p. 106.

9 Paula Casey, "ADR Comes to the Courthouse," *Washington State Bar News,* March 1996, at p. 26.

10 Jerome Wolf and Kent Snapp, "Novel 'Early Assessment Program' Cuts Costs," *National Law Journal,* April 29, 1996, at p. B-9.

11 See Ellen Joan Pollock, "Mediation Firms Alter the Legal Landscape," *Wall Street Journal,* March 22, 1993, at p. B-1.

12 Barry Meier, "In Fine Print, Customers Lose the Ability to Sue," *New York Times,* March 10, 1997, at p. A-1.

13 See CPR Institute for Dispute Resolution, *ADR Cost Savings and Benefits Studies,* New York, 1994.

14 See Deloitte & Touche Litigation Services, "Survey of General and Outside Counsels," Chicago, 1993, at p. 1.

15 Jane Birnbaum, "Guilty! Too Many Lawyers and Too Much Litigation. Here Is a Better Way," *Business Week,* April 13, 1992, at p. 60.

16 CPR Report p. I-24.

17 Ibid, p. I-33.

18 "Food Concerns Opt to Mediate, Not Litigate," *Wall Street Journal,* February 11, 1993, at p. B-1.

19 See Margaret A. Jacobs, "Arbitration and the Like Attract More Converts and Revenue at Firms," *Wall Street Journal,* February 24, 1995, at p. B-8.

20 Rhonda McMillon, "Growing Acceptance for ADR," *ABA Journal,* May 1996, at p. 106.

21 See American Bar Association, *ABA Blueprint for Improving the Civil Justice System: Report of the American Bar Association's Working Group on Civil Justice System Proposals,* Chicago, 1992, at pp. 31-35.

22 Kirk Johnson, "Public Judges as Private Contractors: A Legal Frontier," *New York Times,* December 10, 1993, at p. B-11.

23 See Linda M. Roubik, "Non-Attorneys Should Not Mediate Financial Issues in Family Law Cases," *Bar Bulletin of the King County Bar Association,* May 1996, at pp. 14-15.

24 Henry J. Reske, "Downward Trends," *ABA Journal,* December 1996, at p. 24.

25 See Brookings Institution, *Charting a Future for the Civil Justice System: Report of an American Bar Association/Brookings Institution Symposium* (Washington, DC: Brookings Institution, 1992).

26 See Federal Judicial Center, *Planning for the Future: Results of a 1992 Federal Judiciary Center Survey of United States Judges,* Washington, DC, 1994.

27 See James Podgers, "Changes Sought in Civil Justice System," *ABA Journal,* February 1994, at p. 111.

28 Darryl Van Duch, "Case Management Reform Ineffective," *National Law Journal,* February 3, 1997, at p. A-6.

29 Darryl Van Duch and Marcia Coyle, "Start Over on Case Management Reform?" *National Law Journal,* February 10, 1997, at p. A-6.

30 Dean Starkman, "Judges' Authority to Slash Fees Demanded by Lawyers Expands," *Wall Street Journal,* November 20, 1996, at p. B-11.

31 Mike France, "Cake for Lawyers, Crumbs for Clients," *Business Week,* April 29, 1996, at p. 86.

32 *BMW v. Gore,* 116 S. Ct. 1589, 134 L. Ed. 2d 809 (1996).

33 Henry J. Reske, "Guidelines Instead of Bright Lines," *ABA Journal,* July 1996, at p. 36.

34 Quoted in Max Boot, "The Mass Tort That Wasn't," *Wall Street Journal,* November 6, 1996, at p. A-23.

35 See Daniel W. Shuman, Anthony Champagne, and Elizabeth Whitaker, "Juror Assessments of the Believability of Expert Witnesses: A Literature Review," *Jurimetrics Journal* 36:4 (Summer 1996), at pp. 372-382.

36 Ibid, at p. 372.

37 President's Council on Competitiveness, *Agenda for Civil Justice Reform: A Report from the President's Council on Competitiveness* (Washington, DC: GPO, 1991), at p. 4.

38 See ABA, *Blueprint*, at pp. 79-81 and appendix.

39 *Frye v. United States*, 293 F. 1013 (D.C. 1923).

40 See Barry Meier, "Judges Set Up Review Panel for Lawsuits on Implants, *New York Times,* April 4, 1996, at p. A-12 and Richard B. Schmitt, "Panel of Experts to Study Breast Implants," *Wall Street Journal,* June 3, 1996, at p. B-2.

41 *Markman v. Westview Instruments,* 116 S. Ct. 1384, 134 L. Ed. 2d 577 (1996).

42 Linda Greenhouse, "High Court Gives Jury's Role in Complex Patents to Judge," *New York Times,* April 24, 1996, at p. A-1.

43 *Daubert v. Merrell Dow Pharmaceuticals,* 113 S. Ct. 2786, 125 L. Ed. 2d 469 (1993). See also Paul Reidinger, "They Blinded Me with Science!" *ABA Journal,* September 1996, at pp. 58-62.

44 See Max Boot, op cit, and Kathryn Kranhold, "Judges Seen Getting Tough on Scientific Evidence, *Wall Street Journal,* November 27, 1996, at p. A-1.

45 "Are Special Courts the Future?" *Business Law Today,* Jan/Feb 1995, at p. 25.

46 See "A Commercial Venture," *ABA Journal,* January 1996, at p. 35; Mike France, "Order in the Business Court," *Business Week,* December 9, 1996, at p. 138; and Robert L. Haig, "New York Creates Business Courts," *Business Law Today,* Sept/Oct 1996, at p. 31. For a more scholarly analysis, see Rochelle C. Dreyfuss, "Forums of the Future: The Role of Specialized Courts in Resolving Business Disputes," *Brooklyn Law Review* 61:1 (1995), at pp. 1- 43 and Jeffrey W. Stempel, "Two Cheers for Specialization," *Brooklyn Law Review* 61:67 (1995) at pp. 67 - 128.

CHAPTER FOUR
REFORM

L et's fast-forward to the year 2020.
To a study, actually: "Vision 2020: Building a Strategic Plan for Colorado Courts."[1] This project, which was conceived by the Colorado Supreme Court's Judicial Advisory Council and produced by the Colorado Judicial Department, undertook to identify the major trends that would influence Colorado's courts. Five were identified:

- Substantial population growth and aging.
- Continued increases in social diversity and corresponding frictions and conflicts.
- Continuing economic polarization, generating increased criminal and civil caseloads.
- Continuing changes in the definition and composition of the family, increasing the court system's role in protecting women, children, and families "from abuses that result from the economic and emotional stresses of such change."
- The Information Revolution. The project saw this trend as "perhaps [the] most important for the judicial system." Among the expected effects was an increase in litigation, due to greater complexity in society and greater diffusion of legal information. The project also anticipated that some technological advances would create new le-

gal problems, while others would offer solutions, perhaps in as-yet undefinable ways.

The project then used these trends to determine what kind of justice system the state of Colorado might require in 2020. It found that civil justice would become more "consumer-oriented." The report explained that "the intent of the [civil] legal system will no longer be adversarial, but will seek to find mutually agreeable solutions to problems." Also, lawyers no longer will be the only professionals involved in dispute resolution, and will receive multidisciplinary training so that they are better qualified to meet a goal of "fair dispute resolution, not winning and losing."

To attain these goals, the report recommended consolidating various county courts into a single trial court system that would operate through "neighborhood justice centers." These would offer trial and ADR services, and maintain a staff to counsel disputants on their options. The report also recommended stronger case management standards to deal with present-day procedural excesses and abuses. The project, whose participants included judges and lawyers, concluded that the bar itself must take a more active role in assuring that its members understand their redefined duties and have the necessary tools to fulfill them. The public must be made more knowledgeable about the law, and lawyers must accept that their "public responsibilities sometimes override personal, as well as client, interests."

Now shift to a kindred study: *Alternative Futures for the State Courts of 2020*, published by the State Justice Institute and the American Judicature Society. This exercise in quasi-whimsical legal futurism offers a number of scenarios, written from the perspective of the year 2020. They tend, as futurist scenarios often do, toward the fanciful. Still, two merit attention here:

"Multi-Door Courthouse" and "Global High-Tech."

The first exercise in judicial prophecy conjured up a system that combined ADR and adversary procedures. This came about because of the growing popularity of ADR. But it also prevailed because "many jurists who might well have *preferred* to have all matters decided in the traditional adversarial way came to champion ADR simply as a means to keep the formal system alive and able to function in at least the most important areas where the age-old majesty of the adversarial courts was felt to be imperative."[2] The scenario also noted that "multi-door" fit "multicultural" better than "adversarial."

The other scenario, "Global High-Tech," predicted the effects of Information Age technologies on traditional justice, and dwelt upon the inexorable nature of the forces behind those effects:

"So, we let the nose of the camel in under the edge of the tent. We brought in technology, which permitted lawyers to file cases from their offices. Menu-driven, this software did not need someone to explain how to fill out the form, or to ridicule you when you did it wrong. And you don't have to hand-carry it and wait in line for a clerk to slam the window on your fingers at 4:29 PM. The form was electronically 'corrected' and instantly dispatched and registered, 24 hours a day. Once you were on-line, you had access to data banks of all sorts. . . .

"Centuries of judicial decisions were not only collected on data bases like WESTLAW and LEXIS, but also were fully relational. Litigants could enter the facts of their case into any convenient AJM (Automated Justice Machine) and receive instant justice based on the facts of similar cases previously decided. . .

"The electronic camel slid in effortlessly. In the 1980s, there was considerable case backlog. Computers helped eliminate it. Determining the standing of claimants in worldwide product liability cases nearly overwhelmed certain civil courts until computer modeling techniques were utilized. . . . Some of the first judicial decision-making computer models were developed by law firms to allow attorneys to predict case resolutions and then decide on whether to file, settle, or drop cases.

"Same-day hearings, made possible by computers, were first applied to certain traffic cases . . .

"In certain cases at first, juries were electronically pre-selected and reviewed by opposing attorneys and then heard cases without ever being brought physically together . . . many judges were recruited from the scientific and technological fields . . . costs of litigation were dropping rapidly . . ."[3]

Whether this scenario comes to pass in its entirety is debatable. However, the judicial survey cited in the previous chapter, the Colorado project, and the imaginative *Alternative Futures*, all point to the general direction in which I believe the civil justice system should move. First, recognize the present problems, needs, and opportunities. Second, reorganize the courts. And third, begin to investigate and deploy the Information Age technologies that will form and affect the law just as profoundly as the transition from oral to written law, and from the written to the printed word.

When I wrote the first draft of this book, I did not intend to offer a prescription for a 21st century court system. Such theorizing seemed to me presumptuous. I'm no prophet. Nor am I a techno-determinist, convinced that computers will bring us either perdition or paradise. Nor am I an academic legal scholar or professional ethicist. I'm a practicing attorney who also is trained in the anthropological art of observing the present.

Nonetheless, those who read the book's first draft demanded that I put a stake in the ground. To criticize and leave it at that, they said, was inadequate and perhaps intellectually dishonest.

117

I had to offer my views, for whatever they might be worth.

I got the opportunity to set down some thoughts in, of all places, Katmandu, Nepal. I had gone with my husband on a trekking vacation, tore a tendon, and had to be taken back to a hotel. There I reverted to my anthropological habits, observing both the locals and the guests. I met a surprising number of business people of varied nationalities whose work routinely takes them all over the world. While waiting for the trekking group to return, I had a chance to write with pen and paper, sitting in the lobby of an old hotel in a city that is still trying to build a satisfactory garbage system, but boasts seven television stations and an ever-growing number of computers to connect their Nepalese owners over the Internet with a world their grandparents may not have even known existed. And it occurred to me there that I had to write about the future for no other reason than that the future is already here.

And it is a future in which geography is yielding to cyberspace; in which the hegemonies of dominant groups are yielding (for good or ill) to a mixing of deities and peoples; and in which old ways of binding us together and resolving our differences must give way to new. To believe that change stops with us is presumptuous. To believe that the future will be easy is naïve. To believe that it can be evaded by refusal to think about it is ridiculous.

In trying to sketch a future legal system, I was confronted by three facts of life in late 20th century America. The first is that as Americans have become more tolerant and accepting of diversity, and as law has come to give special status to certain differences, it has become more difficult to define a single set of shared "American" values. This affects the legal system, inasmuch as there is a vital link between a society's collective values and its laws. Moreover, one of the theoretical arguments in favor of the lay jury is that, whenever law deviates too greatly from community values, the jury can "nullify" the law. But this too assumes that at least a minimal set of community values can be articulated. As Jethro Lieberman writes in *The Litigious Society*:

"The litigious impulse lies deeper than greed. A lawsuit is a signal that something has gone wrong. It may be a little thing – like the refusal of a person to abide by a promise. Or it may be a major failure: the impotence of political institutions, the disequilibrium of an economy, the decay of social organizations, the collapse of corporate competence, the decline of communal feeling.

"From this perspective, litigiousness may be viewed not only as a signal of failure but also as a clarion of social health. For the willingness to go to court is a sign that we are not going to the streets – the court of last resort."[4]

There is a certain truth here. Still, our task is not to celebrate the uses of litigation *in extremis*. The job is to craft a legal system that will set right that which has gone wrong internally and also respond to that which has gone wrong – and is going right – in the larger society. Obviously, this grows harder as society becomes more complex and decentralized, technologically, socially, and culturally. One of the great challenges of the 21st century will be to define and maintain a set of American values that can bring some commonality, if not uniformity, to a multitude of thriving subcultures.

Ultimately, any legal system must address the relationship between the needs, wants, and desires of the individual and those of the broader community. But what will that broader community be in the Information Age?

In the past, courtesy of a "melting pot" philosophy and style, there was an expressed, even if not always real, uniformity among Americans. Assimilation to some sort of middle-class ideal was the way it was supposed to be. Those who hadn't made it were at least expected to try. Popular acceptance of such uniformity may have been a mile wide and an inch deep in some ways. But at least it allowed for a definable set of values, ostensibly shared by most members of the majority culture and significant portions of minority cultures, which could be reflected in the legal system. This set of values, derived from the 18th century Enlightenment and its 19th century progeny, classical liberalism, was reinforced by America's Judeo-Christian underpinnings . . . and by the economic imperatives of a capitalist consumer society. The majority culture "owned" and was "owned by" all three.

Today, we have a greater appreciation and respect for different cultural values and rules. We have become more aware that the values and rules that govern life for ghetto gangs or ecological communes or religious sects can differ in many ways from the values and rules that govern life in an upper-middle-class suburb. Today, people are expected to celebrate and intensify their differences, be they linguistic, religious, racial, ethnic, or sexual. For many, one's "affinity group" provides a more meaningful identity than one's citizenship.

This difference in values struck me with special force during the O.J. Simpson trial. Over and over, when female African Americans were asked to comment, they expressed their regret that another African American male might be going to prison for a long time. This provided a stark contrast to the reactions of Caucasian women, who focused on Mr. Simpson's innocence or guilt.

Many years ago, anthropologist Richard Adams taught me the importance of cultural values. Dr. Adams showed me that individuals and cultures create hierarchies of values and make decisions based upon the relative importance of the values involved. To speak of shared values is also to speak of shared hierarchies of values. It is quite conceivable that, to those African American women, the loss through imprisonment of so many male members of that culture might be a greater problem and threat than one individual's innocence or guilt. A 1997 *New Yorker* article on hung juries in criminal trials also noticed this phenomenon. The article pointed out that jurors may refuse to convict because of their own unpleasant past experiences with police and their belief that police "set up" African American males, regardless of the evidence presented in court.[5]

This does not mean that these women and men regard innocence and guilt as unimportant or irrelevant. It does mean that they placed those items within the larger context of the health and future of the African American community, as they understood that community's situation, prospects, and needs. Whatever the "shared" values related to the taking of human life and other criminal deeds, the subgroup value of protecting a specific community could not be denied. Thus, for better or worse, the legal system must find ways to address competing hierarchies of value while maintaining the civil order necessary for us all to survive.

From a 21st century perspective, our richly variegated culture can be a source of strength in the jury box. However, if the evidence is so complex and technical that jurors cannot understand it, this strength becomes a weakness. When jurors cannot grasp the evidence, they have scant recourse save to base their decisions on criteria having little or nothing to do with the dispute at hand – criteria such as race, gender, the lawyers' theatrics, even their (and their clients') clothing or hair. If jurors vote on the basis of purely personal preferences or subcultural affiliation because they are unable to vote on the basis of the evidence, then the very diversity that could be a source of strength becomes a curse, undermining the jury's vital role within the adversary system. The goal must be diverse juries that can evaluate the evidence objectively and decide accordingly.

A second observation, which struck me so forcefully in Katmandu and daily when considering my own company's work force, is that geography is becoming less important in defining one's society and group. It is not just that global migration and travel have become so prevalent. The electronic media are blurring the connection between national and cultural borders. Cyberspace is completing the job. Communication on the Internet has virtually nothing to do with geography.

This change is profound, if not yet fully understood . . . at least in part because it's too easily over-hyped or condemned. Obviously, the Internet will never replace personal contact entirely, any more than the telephone or the Postal Service did. But the Internet creates enormous new options and potentialities for human interaction. Early computers permitted people to do things they had always done, only faster and more efficiently. Now computers permit us to do things we have never done before. The Internet is not merely a faster way of moving information from point to point. It creates new political, social and cultural forms, in the process rendering the old ones not necessarily archaic or useless, but certainly far less powerful and exclusive.

Consider the simple fact of geography. As an old proverb puts it, "Everybody has to be somewhere." Still true, at the purely physical level. But the purely physical level is no longer the only plane upon which humans interact. And these new planes are profoundly different from the physical. In the past, when human contact was shaped by proximity or prohibited by distance, geography provided demarcation lines as clear as those of race, religion or ethnicity. But on the Internet, it is often impossible to define others by these boundaries, or to defend or set up boundaries against them. All the old cues – names, addresses, clothing, accents – are gone. We define relationships on other bases that need not include physical points of reference at all.

The American legal system, however, is still based on geography – local courts, state courts, federal courts, each defined by its jurisdiction over legal matters and individuals within a prescribed geographical area. Similarly, international legal forums have been designed to deal with disputes across physical boundaries.[6]

But what will happen as geography becomes an ever less relevant manner of arranging courts and administering justice? What forums will be appropriate to address wrongs that occur in cyberspace? And as international courts become more important, what roles will, or should, local and national courts play? Business and communications have been internationalized beyond recall. What will happen as "society" itself becomes less geographically-based? For decades, marketing and political analysts have known that populations could be divided along psychographic (grouping by psychological traits), "life-style," and "affinity" as well as geographical lines . . . and that, for their purposes, these divisions might be more useful. A retired school teacher or adolescent punk rocker or gay person in, say, New York, may have more in common with his or her "life-style" counterpart in Seattle or Dubuque than with the neighbors down the street. The legal implications of nontraditional "affinity groups" – the affiliations one chooses – have yet to be addressed in any systematic way.

A third observation is that Americans have grown too eager to translate grievances into money, especially in an era when nobody seems to be without his or her repertoire of grievances.

Although the legal system permits courts to grant non-monetary or "equitable" relief, it is far more common for plaintiffs to seek, and for courts to grant, "damages" – monetary compensation for woes which may never have entailed the loss of a single dime. Why do we ask courts, for example, to assign a monetary value to the loss of "consortium," i.e., to the loss of the company of one's spouse? Punitive damages are the ultimate example. Money is granted the plaintiff in order to punish the defendant, not to compensate for monetary or even non-monetary losses.

It can, of course, be argued that money is the one "universal value" in this society, and "get it any way you can" expresses that value's creed. But this cynical, materialistic perception does not mean that civil justice must be measured or rendered in purely monetary terms. Indeed, to the extent that the "monetizing of grievance" forces the system to focus on money, not the rectification of wrongs or the resolution of disputes, it demeans and debases the legal system. The work of a justice system should be less mercenary and more noble: keeping order among individuals for the good of the whole.

As noted earlier, many now criticize the legal profession for becoming too greedy and businesslike. Few find lawyers' obsession with "size of verdict" healthy, for the profession, the judicial system, or the society they serve. But if civil justice has come to be about money, no wonder too many attorneys seem to think first and foremost about how much cash they can carry away.

All of which brings us to a view of what the civil justice system of the 21st century should look like. Again, this view is colored by certain assumptions concerning technology's relentless advance, society's centrifugal tendencies, and the obsolescence of the present system. These may prove to be wrong in some particulars. But I am convinced that they're correct enough to justify serious consideration of reforms which may seem radical in the present context, though also logical enough when viewed across the centuries of the legal system's historical development.

THE SYSTEM

In the introduction to this book, I offered a name to describe the kind of courts which, I believe, would be most responsive to the needs and values of the future. I called them CORE Courts, an acronym standing for "COmmonality/REsolution" – COmmonality of subject-matter, with emphasis on REsolution of disputes. The time has come to develop this idea – a concept that combines venerable principles and practices with 21st century technology.

Briefly stated, I see the civil justice system of the 21st century as an integrated structure of CORE Courts that will be organized according to subject-matter. This organization distinguishes it from the current system of courts of "general jurisdiction" – generalist courts that hear, on a more or less random basis, cases that crisscross the range of human experience.

Another key difference between CORE Courts and the current generalist system is that CORE Courts will integrate ADR within the traditional adversary system. Each CORE Court will offer both informal and formal ADR forums, in addition to adversarial trials. Each CORE Court will adopt and operate under those rules of procedure which best fit its unique subject-matter jurisdiction. Constitutional principles and protections will, of course, continue to apply, and the U.S. Supreme Court and state-level courts of highest resort will continue to fulfill their constitutionally-defined legal functions.

WHY CREATE A *CORE* COURT SYSTEM BASED ON SUBJECT-MATTER?

Life has become very complex in the Information Age. There is now a superabundance of information, much of it bewilderingly technical and intricate. People in all fields have had to focus their endeavors ever more tightly. Take medicine, for example. It's all specialties now: cardiology, radiology, pediatrics, to name only a few. Even the old GP – "General Practitioner" – is a specialist today, a "family doctor." Engineers, to use another example, have specialized by media. Wireless engineers differ from software engineers, who differ from nuclear engineers and civil and aerospace engineers.

Specialization has certainly captured the practice of law. A quarter-century ago, the vast majority of American lawyers were generalists who could draft wills one day, contracts the next, perhaps argue in court the next. This was, in large measure, due to the fact that information was still relatively sparse and easy to process. But with the dawning of the Information Age, many lawyers, especially those who practiced in the larger locales, found they could no longer function competently as generalists. The individual attorney simply couldn't stay abreast of all the developments in contract law, civil procedure law, real property law, and so forth. And if the individual lawyer could not keep up with developments within the profession, what chance did he or she have to stay on top of changes in the multitude of industries and activities important to the clients?

At first, specialization within the legal profession was simple. There were litigators who went to court and non-litigators whose practices usually did not involve courtroom time. But inevitably, lawyers diversified into many more subgroups. Today, the American Bar Association is divided into more than twenty "sections," defined by their subject-matter. Thus we now have family lawyers, securities lawyers, commercial lawyers, patent lawyers, criminal lawyers, copyright lawyers, real property lawyers, entertainment lawyers, personal injury lawyers, estate planning lawyers, tax lawyers, labor lawyers, and many other specialists. Some of these subfields didn't even exist a few decades ago. Environmental law, for example, is a relative newcomer. And who knows what specialties have yet to arise or assume their full importance? Outer space lawyers, for example, or cyberspace lawyers?

But because our courts have remained generalist, today we have a serious disconnection between the world outside the courtroom and the world inside. We bring specialist lawyers into the courtroom to talk to judges and juries who, by and large, have remained generalists. Indeed, one part of the system absolutely demands generalists. Jurors are supposed to be the ultimate generalists, "blank slates" who theoretically know nothing save what the lawyers tell them through the witnesses. (The dismal fact that jurors are now routinely chosen for their prejudices as well as their ignorance only exacerbates the problem.)

This gap between real-world specialization and judicial generalism is, I believe, a significant contributor to the growing sense of injustice and unfairness in our courts. Justice requires that the legal system operate on the basis of reality, not dysfunction justified by theory. The reality is that human experience has grown far more diverse, and knowledge far more complex and specialized, than even 25 years ago – less than the length of my own career. So it's time for the courts to do what so many lawyers have had to do: specialize, the better to understand and process the information that is so important to the litigants. After all, one of the primary functions of the adversary system is to let the litigants get their information to the decision-makers. But if the decision-makers cannot understand what the litigants and witnesses are saying, then the adversary system has been compromised at best, and at worst rendered useless.

Therefore, the CORE Courts will have decision-makers who possess at least some familiarity with the relevant subject matter. This familiarity can be acquired through academic and practical experience, and through court-based training and experience. Court-appointed experts may also help provide some of the relevant background knowledge that will allow the decision-makers to do their jobs more effectively.

Two final introductory points, and a set of caveats:

First, CORE Courts are not revolutionary. Legal history – certainly, American legal history – shows that a purely generalist court system meets the needs of only the most rudimentary societies.[7] No complex society has a purely generalist system. We don't. The current court system, though primarily composed of courts of general jurisdiction, also incorporates subject-matter courts: tax and bankruptcy courts, family and juvenile courts, and military courts, to name a few. The Federal Circuit, established to decide patent cases, is a specialized court. The Delaware Business Court offers a recent example. I propose that we now need a civil justice system in which subject-matter courts are more the rule than the exception.

Second, it is not necessary to do away with all geographically-based courts. The court system still must be administered through governments that, whether national, state, or local, are based upon geography. Moreover, in some locales, the neighborhood does represent a real community of interest, where the litigants and decision-makers still share a common base of knowledge and experience. A friend who practices in a semi-rural, two-person law firm made this point clear to me recently. Unlike his urban colleagues, he still practices in all areas of the law. Yet he's a specialist. His specialty is the domain of his small town, which still functions as a relatively closed community. He knows all about the local industries and economy, and all about the people of the town. So do the judge and the town's few other lawyers. Precisely because they know their territory so well, these lawyers and the judge have neither been subjected to, nor have they taken up, the kinds of adversary system abuses now so common in larger towns and cities.

And there may be an additional benefit to non-geographic courts. Where geographic communities have lost their cohesion, or grown hostile, support for the legal system is eroded. Non-geographic courts, by bypassing at least some of this indifference and/or hostility, can command more respect than might otherwise be the case.

That said, it is important to note that increased use of specialized courts has been proposed before, and that such proposals have encountered a more or less standardized set of objections.[8] The gravamen is that, although specialized courts do offer advantages of efficiency and expertise, they also undermine justice by being too low in stature, too insulated, and too isolated. I suggest that these are problems to be addressed, not insurmountable obstacles.

Traditionally, specialty courts have had a lesser legal status than courts of general jurisdiction, and have tended to attract (at least according to some observers) a lower quality of judge. By this reasoning, high-quality judges prefer courts of general jurisdiction because they find them more challenging and less boring than narrow, presumably repetitive specialties.

Another argument is that a specialist system provides too narrow an experiential base for sound decision-making. In a generalist court, cases may "cross-fertilize" – judges may bring laws, ideas, and theories from one area to others.

And yet another point is that a specialty system, because of its greater efficiency and predictability, might actually harm the development of law. In a generalist system, cases "percolate" for longer periods in the lower courts before reaching the Supreme Court. This means that, on issues of great national and constitutional significance, there would be more work done and understanding gained prior to final judgment.

These objections are not without a certain resonance. However, they fall short in two ways. First, they argue more from theory and abstraction than from reality. Legal scholar Jeffrey W. Stempel describes this phenomenon as "the tendency to overmodel" and concludes: "The [current] boundary between specialized and generalist courts, however, is not nearly so bright as commonly assumed."[9]

Clearly, lawyers have not, as a profession, become unbearably bored by specialization. Many find it exhilarating, especially in the newer and more complex fields, such as telecommunications and environmental law. Is there any compelling reason to believe that judges are that different from lawyers in their ability to derive personal and professional satisfaction from more specialized tasks? And is there any reason to believe that CORE Courts handling some of the most important cases around will have less prestige than generalist forums? The reverse might well be more likely.

Second, the problem of cross-fertilization becomes far less severe when the nature of specialization is broadened, as it would be in the CORE Courts. These would not be narrow "cookie-cutter" forums. Many cases would have great relevance outside their own areas, and there is no reason why considerations in one CORE Court could not apply to and in others.

Finally, it is a venerable notion in law that cases should be "ripe for judgment," especially if they have constitutional significance. But there is no arbitrary amount of time that "ripens" any particular case. In the fast-moving Information Age, "ripening" cases for years and years may be unnecessary, impractical, and unfair.

Now, to develop the proposal.

HOW MANY DIFFERENT *CORE* COURTS WILL THERE BE?

The simple answer is, as few or as many as necessary. And these will very likely change over time, as subject areas grow more complicated and perhaps split into new areas, and as totally new specialties arise. For the immediate future, a system of CORE Courts might roughly parallel the current system of law practice specialties, perhaps using the ABA's section structure as a guide.

Thus, to take an easy example, family matters such as divorce and adoption would be resolved in the Family CORE Court. Many jurisdictions already have Family Courts, so this would not be an extreme change. At a more complex level, the CORE Court system might encompass one or more Commercial Courts, or an Entertainment Court, or a Communications Court. The CORE Court system could be structured around industry types (medical, biotechnical, automotive, publishing, broadcasting, computing, etc.) or perhaps by type of claim (employment-related, sales-related, warranty-related, etc.). In the torts area, claims arising from traffic accidents might go to one CORE Court, while professional malpractice cases might go to another. The point is that, in all cases, CORE Courts would be characterized by some unity of subject-matter focus. With such subject-matter focus as the *leitmotif*, CORE Courts could be organized in many different ways. Probably, some types of disputes might fit more than one subject-matter court. For example, would a case involving piracy of on-line entertainment material go to Computer Court or Intellectual Property Court? Might "venue-shopping" (looking for the most favorable forum) become a problem?

Perhaps. But again, these are factors to be considered in constructing the system, not fatal defects. And, to repeat a final time, subject-matter courts are far from new. They are the courts appropriate to complex societies. They've worked well in the past; they work well today.

In addition to problems related to system construction, two obvious objections may be raised. The first is that such courts will be susceptible to abuse or "capture" by persons or groups with particular interests or agendas. This objection is hardly new. It is raised recurrently by those dissatisfied with decision-making by specialized administrative agencies, such as the Federal Trade Commission, Food and Drug Administration, Social Security, and Worker's Compensation, to name only a few. But this objection, like the problems of overlap and venue-shopping, is really more a legitimate worry, inseparable from the facts of life in any judicial forum, than an unanswerable argument against CORE Courts. And, as Stempel points out, "Generalist courts are at least as susceptible to political influence as specialist courts, even though in theory specialist courts are more vulnerable. . . . [W]e do not yet know enough about interest group influence on different systems. However, nominations to the bankruptcy court and the Federal Circuit [which handles patent cases] have been no more marred than generalist judicial selection by the self-interested participation of academics, the patent bar, the creditor bar, banks, other lenders, manufacturers and ideologues generally."[10]

Caution is needed, obviously. But it is a caution no different than that required by the present set of generalist courts.

The second objection, that the CORE Court system would be too complex, is more serious. As one who favors simplicity over complexity, I generally resist complicated structures. But the growing complexity of day-to-day life, fueled by ever greater access to more of everything – people, cultures, knowledge, technology – requires more diversification. Just as the Industrial Era required a more complicated and integrated set of roads than the Agrarian Era, and just as contemporary aviation requires a far more complex system of routes and regulations than it did in the barnstorming days, so there must be a more complex civil justice system for the Information Age. Both simplicity and complexity can facilitate human interaction. It all depends on what needs to be done. CORE Courts will accommodate both the growing breadth of human activity and the exponentially growing depth of information applicable to every area of activity.

HOW WILL THE CORE COURT SYSTEM BE ADMINISTERED?

The current system essentially comprises federal and state courts. The jurisdiction of the federal courts is not limited solely to questions of federal law. Similarly, the courts of one state are not precluded from deciding questions involving the laws of another state. The U.S. Supreme Court, of course, has ultimate responsibility for deciding matters of constitutional importance.

The CORE Courts will be overseen by governmental bodies, although the pattern of oversight will be more complex than the simple federal/state model. Which governmental body oversees a particular CORE Court will depend on the subject-matter of that court. Again, to use an easy example, Family CORE Courts probably would be supervised by the states; most family law issues, such as adoption and divorce, are matters of state law.

Commercial issues, on the other hand, are increasingly inter-state in nature. CORE Courts dealing with these issues might more logically be overseen by federal authorities.

However, entirely new forms of oversight might be neces-sary or useful. For example, a regional body might be appropri-ate to oversee some CORE Courts, while new types of international bodies might be created to oversee CORE Courts dealing with matters of international concern, such as tariffs or environmental regulation. This could be an extremely delicate undertaking, given concerns about possible infringements of national sovereignty.

These oversight bodies would, within constitutional and other applicable legislative restrictions and guidance (including rel-evant provisions of treaties), determine the procedures and rules of the CORE Courts under their jurisdiction. These would prob-ably vary from court to court. This is critical to making CORE Courts function properly. Rules of procedure in a Family CORE Court, for example, might well differ from those in an Intellec-tual Property CORE Court.

This new system will undoubtedly take time to develop, as jurists and legislators attempt to determine what Courts there should be, and who will oversee them. In a sense, the process will never end, can never end. But there is nothing new about changing realities leading to changes in law.

How Will the ADR and The Adversary Systems Be Integrated?

If nothing else, current court congestion demonstrates the need for third-party dispute resolvers. This need will grow be-cause our society is more centrifugal and more individualistic than it used to be, and because of the trend noted by Bill Ide and

George Will toward expecting the law to do more of what church, family, and other mediating institutions once did. Because of this loss of mediating institutions, the need for legal and quasi-legal forums will increase even if people begin to grow less brutishly confrontational and litigious. It also will continue because of accelerating globalization and attendant economic and social stresses.

These trends do not necessarily mandate more judges and juries. The ADR phenomenon strongly indicates that, so long as the disputants believe that an arbitrator or mediator will act responsibly and objectively, the third party's actions and decisions will be respected and followed. In some cases, these decision-makers will be judges and jurors. In others, they will be judges only, and in yet others they may be mediators or other non-judicial dispute resolvers. The "mix" of facilities will develop over time. Again, the point is to let the substance of the issues at hand determine what combination of ADR and adversarial components will be necessary.

And there is another reason, already mentioned, for integrating judicial and ADR systems. If ADR operates entirely outside the court system, the development of the common law will be seriously impeded, perhaps even jeopardized. They must be integrated – a recommendation also found in the Colorado "Vision 2020" study.

In essence, the CORE Court system would operate in a manner similar to that envisioned by the Colorado study. Disputants would come to the CORE Court and would be directed (according to the rules of the Court and with full protection for the parties' constitutional right to jury trial) along different resolution paths, depending on the nature of the dispute. The Court itself will include under its umbrella an integrated system of forums, ranging from ADR to juryless trials before one or perhaps a panel of judges, to full-blown jury trials, then perhaps to an appellate division. As part of the integration of ADR and the adversary system, CORE Court administrators will address the issue of how to handle disputes that are best resolved by ADR, but that also present questions relevant to the development of the common law. Such disputes may be subject to a resolution procedure that uses a judge instead of an arbitrator and that combines certain features of ADR and certain features of a trial. The goal is to let the substance of the issues at hand determine what type of forum would be best suited for a timely and effective resolution from the vantage point of both the litigants and the larger society.

WHAT HAPPENS TO THE ADVERSARY SYSTEM IN THE CORE COURTS?

Answering this question requires that, once again, we distinguish between the adversary system as it should be and the adversary system as we have come to know it. From the vantage point of the former, the adversary system will be refreshed and renewed by the CORE Courts. From the perspective of the latter, the CORE Courts will entail a major restructuring.

The three elements of the classic adversary system will all be preserved in the CORE Courts.

First, the CORE Court system will retain the parties' right to present their cases directly to adversary system decision-makers, up to and including full trials. About the responsibilities of lawyers and clients, more in a moment.

The second element of the system, the decision-makers, will change significantly. In the CORE Court system, the judge and jury will remain neutral. But they will not be totally passive. In some courts, they may be very active. *And they will not be igno-*

rant. In this respect, they may actually resemble judges and juries of the past, where both litigants and decision-makers shared a common base of knowledge.

The neutral and passive requirement has to be viewed in its historical context. In the late 18th century, and well into the 20th century, when communities were relatively small and culturally more unified, a neutral and passive juror walked into the courtroom with a sense of the shared values extant in his local society. Moreover, in most small communities, he would likely come into the courtroom with some prior knowledge and perhaps even an opinion about the parties to a case, perhaps even about the issue to be litigated. And he would have to live within the community after the trial ended. From an anthropological perspective, these shared values and opinions can be seen as essential parts of the community's "social contract." The jurors' decisions "objectively" reinforced local values in the resolution of the community's disputes.

But in our contemporary society, we are harder pressed to find a uniform set of shared values. This diversity of perspectives is one of the reasons jury consultants have become so popular. It is also one of the reasons commentators and scholars decry the politicization of modern juries. This diversity is a fact of life, and the task is not to pass judgment on it, but to find better ways to resolve disputes in a healthy and satisfactory manner.

To do this, we must recover at least a minimal quantity and quality of shared experience and knowledge between litigant and decision-maker. It may not be possible to do this based upon geographical proximity. Few people live their entire adult lives in one small locale anymore. In the context of civil justice, it may be more useful to base the concept of "shared experience" more upon the subject of the dispute and less upon where the dispute occurs. The decision-makers have to be able to understand what the litigants are talking about. For that reason, a key feature of the CORE Court is the employment of facilitators and decision-makers who maintain independent knowledge and understanding about the subject-matter that defines their Court's jurisdiction.

This knowledge and understanding may be acquired and maintained in several ways. For judges, it may come through past experience in a given area, as is true today in Tax Court. It may come through training and continuing education, as is true for many Family Court judges today. And it will always come by experience, through the years of hearing cases within each CORE Court's subject-matter purview.

Another way such knowledge and understanding may be acquired is through court-appointed experts who advise and perhaps train both judge and jury. Such experts could be either staff or consulting members of the CORE Court. These experts might testify as witnesses in cases, either in lieu of or in addition to experts hired by the litigants, depending on the particular Court's rules of procedure and evidence.

But what of the jury? Here, an obvious problem arises. Judges are full-time professionals. Jurors come and go, usually for very brief periods. This is the most difficult aspect of getting more subject-matter knowledge and understanding into the courtroom.

Today, jurors are called on a random basis from lists of registered voters. When they receive their jury summons, many Americans immediately seek dismissal on account of jobs, family demands, health, or other permitted excuses. Other prospective jurors appear for duty but then avoid service by demonstrating real or feigned disqualifying prejudices. In addition to these forms of juror "self-selection," judges and lawyers have the right to excuse other jurors on the basis of presumed biases or other inadequacies. Unfortunately, this manner of selecting juries often results in panels of the elderly, the retired, and the unemployed. Critics have long suggested, with no malice or insult intended, that such individuals do not constitute a "jury of peers" to many litigants, especially those involved in complex, high-stakes disputes.

Subject to Constitutional and legislative restrictions, CORE Courts will create jury selection criteria that meet their needs. The qualifications for Family Court undoubtedly will differ from those for Intellectual Property or Telecommunications Court. There are many possible ways to create the necessary jury pools. For example, upon registering to vote, citizens could be asked to list the CORE Courts for which they might qualify. The Courts might maintain lists of citizens previously found qualified by virtue of education, experience, or employment. Or the Courts might simply expand the *voir dire* criteria – the right of counsel to question and challenge potential jurors – to include examinations of baseline subject-matter knowledge and experience. Another possibility is that Courts might obtain juror lists from outside sources, such as schools or businesses.

The point is not to limit the possibilities. Voter lists provide only one option among many. The guiding principle is that juries should be peers in more than some irreducible "one individual is the same as the next" legal sense. In what is sure to be a very complex and diverse 21st century society, the definition of "community" must be refined. Jurors should be drawn from "communities" relevant to the case. This will be an extremely important task.

At this point, let me state that I am not advocating the rebirth of what used to be called "blue-ribbon juries." There will be plenty of room for all citizens to serve as jurors within the CORE Court system. Nor will it be true that, the more complex the subject matter, the more "elitist" the jury pool. With each passing year, there are more female and minority scientists, engineers, business people, doctors. It is hard to imagine that, within a couple decades, jury pools chosen for subject-matter familiarity would not also be roughly representative of other subgroups.

I am not advocating elitism, nor do I expect it to come about. What I am doing is attempting to address a basic fact of the Information Age – none of us, even the most educated, will be able to know it all, or even a fraction of "all," anymore. I have a doctorate and a law degree, but that does not qualify me to understand every area of contemporary endeavor. For me as a juror to try to comprehend and then knowledgeably resolve disputed facts in a case involving biotechnology or aeronautical mechanics would, I believe, be virtually impossible without some training in at least the basic aspects of the relevant sciences. That does not mean, however, that I (or anyone) couldn't comprehend or resolve disputed facts relating to any number of other areas of life.

In this regard, it's important to remember just how recent a phenomenon this Information Revolution really is. Even late in the Industrial Era (say, the 1960s), there were relatively few areas of human interaction that were too complex for most jurors to comprehend. For some of those areas that were, special courts such as Tax Court had already been established. Our ways of life were generally familiar to most of us. Schools taught fairly consistent curricula throughout the country. Office and factory workers had fairly uniform expectations of what their tasks would entail. Family structures across groups were, in general, more similar than not. Today, we no longer share a substantially common base of knowledge, let alone values. The courtroom answer to this problem has been to bring in more expert witnesses, who argue with each other.

This makes no sense. We are now asking lay people to decide which of two or more dueling experts is correct when the task involves understanding evidence that is deemed too technical for people to grasp without expert help. Presenting evidence to a decision-maker who cannot understand it is the same as, and in some cases worse than, presenting no evidence at all.

Another objection may also arise. If we have more knowledgeable decision-makers, do we not leave the courts open to more partiality, even in the absence of political, social and economic agendas? For example, over time, will not the decision-makers in the Telecommunications Court become more biased in favor of the telephone companies? The history of federal regulation of industry, beginning with the railroads in the 19th century, confirms the possibility of this effect. In the diplomatic corps, it's sometimes known as "going native" – identifying so closely with the country and people of one's assignment that the diplomat loses sight of why he or she's there in the first place. And, as already noted, CORE Courts can become magnets for activists and special interests with agendas of their own.

Obviously, this danger must be addressed in structuring the CORE Courts. Judges must be appropriately rotated and subject to strict standards of recusal. Jurors must remain subject to *voir dire*. Court-appointed experts must be evaluated under criteria that take prejudices into consideration. But the fears of partiality, prejudice, and special agendas are only that, fears, and not an insuperable obstacle to creation of the CORE Court system. After all, we already have many specialized courts and administrative decision-making bodies in operation, and, whatever their policy shifts, they have never been irrevocably overcome by prejudice or bias in their operations.

Two final notes on jury personnel. First, our courts today have very different rules about how many jurors are needed to constitute a viable panel, and about what percentage must vote for a decision in order to render a verdict. These differences will also be common among the CORE Courts. I would expect a trend toward smaller juries. I would also expect a trend toward panels of several trial judges in more complex cases.

Second, the kinds of jury reforms mentioned in Chapter Three, such as allowing jurors to take notes during a trial and to ask questions through the judge, are all good methods for helping to ensure that jurors actively understand the information presented to them. They will be used in the CORE Courts. In the present situation, these are necessary reforms that should be implemented as soon as possible in the current court systems.

The third element of the adversary system, the rules of procedure and evidence, will also change. But the changes will return these to their intended use: as tools, not weapons. Each CORE Court will operate on rules which will be crafted in part to meet its unique needs. Rules of procedure and evidence may well vary among the CORE Courts more than they currently vary from federal to state courts, or even from state to state. It is quite possible that, in some CORE Courts, witnesses might appear who would be disqualified in other Courts. Similarly, CORE Courts might vary in rules regarding demonstrative evidence.

The need for specialized procedures derives in part from the abundance of data in the Information Age. In the early years of the adversary system, paper evidence was minimal. Oral testimony was the focus of the trial. As writing and printing grew more prevalent, paper evidence became virtually ubiquitous, and the rules were adjusted to accommodate this development. With the advent of the computer, the copier, and the fax machine, documents have become far longer and far more abundant. This has contributed mightily to the increased time and expense of litigation. Add to this the data on tape, CDs, diskettes, and hard drives. With electronic mail and voice mail, there is a record, discoverable in litigation, of millions of communications that in the past would have left no material trace. We may (or may not) be moving toward a "paperless" society, but going "paperless" will exacerbate rather than solve the problem of information glut in the courts. The solution to this problem lies in procedures and rules that can cull out the most relevant data from the sea of information. In an era of specialization, one-size-fits-all procedures are not likely to suffice. The CORE Court system can, however, craft procedures suited to each Court's subject-matter jurisdiction.

In sum, I believe that the CORE Court system will remain true to the ideals which prompted the evolution of the present adversary system. Indeed, I believe that CORE Courts would be more faithful to those ideals than the present system, and also far better adapted to late 20th and 21st century realities. But logic cannot prevail unaided against the forces of interest and inertia, and against the understandable reluctance to undertake major overhaul of such a fundamental institution as the civil justice system. In order for this reform to come to pass, other things must happen. And other people must get involved. Most importantly, the lawyers and the parties-in-interest – those who spend their professional lives within the system and those who depend upon it for justice – must get involved.

LAWYERS AND CLIENTS

There will be no meaningful reform until two powerful groups – lawyers and their clients – are ready to face up to the reality that our present system cannot provide dependable justice in the 20th century, let alone the 21st. Thus, the first step toward implementation of my (or any) serious proposal is to recognize just how badly the system has deteriorated. We further need to recognize that our legal system does not operate in a vacuum. True, the law must stand for and uphold something greater than the whims or fashions of the moment. But its present structure and processes cannot be mistaken for eternal verities. Every other institution in this society – schools, business, government – has acknowledged these facts and has at least begun to make the adaptation to Information Age, multi-cultural realities. Why should the legal system be exempt?

Moreover, it is time to admit that we are on a very slippery slope. To expect more and more of a dangerously deteriorating system is folly. To regard litigation as a game is to strip it of the sense of justice. To impose exorbitant penalties unjustly is to subject society to arbitrary and capricious tyranny.

People know it. Clients know it. Many judges know it. Deep in their hearts, many lawyers know it. Now, if the legal profession can take the lead by following those who have already grasped it, the legal profession can render this country an invaluable service. If my fellow lawyers, whom I hold in high regard, can shed that trinity of evasions – blind defense, cynical acceptance, and ineffectual self-criticism – the result will benefit the profession, the system, and the country.

Lawyers and judges include within their ranks some of our brightest and most creative citizens. Their greater understanding of the legal system, combined with even a modicum of enlightened self-interest and civic concern, can be a powerful force for effective reform. In recent years, many of the most persuasive and impassioned calls for reform have come from attorneys. But their calls have remained essentially unanswered. At the very least, lawyers and judges can become more proactive in dealing with the game-playing. Judges in particular have the means to curb many of the more egregious abuses. They can assert their authority to manage the cases on their dockets so that substance again becomes more important than process. Judges can also accomplish much through revisions of court rules and procedures.

Lawyers also can act collectively. The ABA and the various state and local bar associations need to lead much more forcefully. To date, most bar association reform proposals have been so watered down (presumably out of a desire to placate everybody) that their usefulness is extremely limited. The leaders of the bar associations must demonstrate that it is possible to take a more proactive, long-term perspective. They must teach their constituencies to do the same. Only then will they fulfill their responsibilities to the legal system and the profession.

In equal measure, legislators must be willing to undertake a good-faith, nonpartisan assessment of the situation, giving serious consideration to the proposals that come before them. Their criteria should be: Does any proposed reform cut down on the game-playing, enhance the likelihood of fair and reasonable resolution of disputes, and reduce the possibilities of abuse?

But perhaps the most immediate good can come from lawyers who choose to incorporate these goals into their own practices now. They can educate their clients as to what is really happening in and to the legal system. Lawyers can also help their clients see that ADR and other cooperative mechanisms may in some cases be the better route toward resolution of a problem. And lawyers can clean up their own acts. They can cut down on the game-playing in their own cases. Perhaps most importantly, lawyers need to stop thinking in "winner takes all" terms and start educating their clients to the desirability of reasonable solutions. Ideally, every law student should graduate with a firm grounding in ADR (not just a vague awareness), as well as knowledge of the social and human sciences that contribute to effective and equitable problem solving. This may take another generation. For the foreseeable future, active attorneys must teach by example. That overworked phrase, "role model," certainly applies here.

For their part, clients and the general public must change their own ways. They need to stop thinking of lawsuits as potential windfalls or basic competitive tools. By the same token, they must stop regarding the settling of predatory lawsuits as a routine cost of business. The same "deep pockets" that make corporations attractive targets also provide the resources to fight. Clients also must remember that they, not their lawyers, are the true parties- in-interest. A client who surrenders control of his or her case to an attorney degrades the attorney/client relationship just as surely as does an attorney who bilks or otherwise misuses a client.

If enough lawyers and enough clients choose to take this high road, and if enough judges back them up, and if enough legislators and pundits pay attention, and if enough law schools catch on, this would be an immensely important first step. But only a first step. For not all the civility and good will in the world can save the present system from obsolescence. Ultimately, we have no choice but to address the impact of the Information Revolution on justice itself, and to implement some fundamental changes in the structure of the civil justice system.

It is now necessary to consider the civil justice system itself as it moves into cyberspace, and the opportunities engendered thereby.

1 A summary can be found in *The Colorado Lawyer,* January 1993, at pp. 11-18.

2 James A. Dator and Sharon J. Rodgers, *Alternative Futures for the State Courts of 2020* (Washington, DC: State Justice Institute and the American Judicature Society, 1991), at p. 28.

3 Ibid, at pp. 37-8.

4 Jethro K. Lieberman, *The Litigious Society* (New York: Basic Books, 1981), at p. 7.

5 Jeffrey Rosen, "One Angry Woman," *New Yorker,* March 3, 1997, at pp. 55-6.

6 For two evocative general and theoretical treatments of the impact of the Information Revolution and cyberspace on law see: M. Ethan Katsch, *Law in a Digital World* (New York: Oxford University Press, 1995) and M. Ethan Katsch, *The Transformation of Law* (New York: Oxford University Press, 1989).

7 For the evolution of courts in pre-Revolutionary America, see Lawrence M. Friedman, *A History of American Law* (New York: Simon & Schuster, 1985), at pp. 17-104.

8 For two useful theoretical analyses of specialty courts, see Rochelle C. Dreyfuss, "Forums for the Future: The Role of Specialized Courts in Resolving Business Disputes," *Brooklyn Law Review* 61:1 (1995), at pp. 1-43 and Jeffrey Stempel, "Two Cheers for Specialization," *Brooklyn Law Review* 61:17 (1995), at pp. 67-128.

9 Stempel, at pp. 89, 91.

10 Ibid, at pp. 97-99, 100-101.

III. Toward justice
in cyberspace

Chapter Five
Final Thoughts and
First Experiments

H istory is, in large measure, the study of change. Our history books are full of lessons about large-scale change, but always with reference to other times and other people – and always neatly packaged into decades or centuries, as though the human beings experiencing those changes did not live them day by bewildering day. Just as we live now.

Traditionally, Americans think of this country as the product of endless, rapid change. This is true. But the changes now upon us are qualitatively different from those that have gone before. Our culture was, almost from the beginning, a product of the Industrial Age. There was no feudal past to sweep away. So while 19th century Europeans had to suffer through the wrenching social changes that followed the invention of the steam engine and its industrial applications – the collapse of extended families, the displacement of populations from rural to urban settings, the development of new philosophical and physical frameworks, and the fundamental reworking of social and economic institutions, including the legal system – we had the luxury of being able to develop without worrying about how to bring a thousand-year-old pre-Industrial past into an Industrial Age future.

But now, in the aftermath of the invention of semiconductor

technology, we are beginning to understand what truly revolutionary change means. In many cases, it means going about our daily business in fundamentally new ways. For many, that can be disorienting, frightening, and something to resist fervently. Even those most directly involved can experience a certain disquietude. In my job at Netscape, I sometimes feel as if I'm sitting in the front of a rocket ship, bound for a world that I can only barely glimpse. The development of the Internet into a worldwide channel of interactive communication is making the nongeographic world of cyberspace a reality. Quite a new frontier. And, as in any frontier, it takes time and experience before the relevant mores, rules, and laws can be fully defined and the appropriate social and economic structures put into place.

In the interim, we frontier people must function with one foot – or, should we say, one part of our minds and spirits – in the old world, and one in the new. The more adventuresome among us try to move forcefully into the new world, but most people probably want to retain as much of the familiar as possible, for as long as possible, i.e., until it becomes obvious that circumstances have simply changed too much. This is the situation today, as we struggle to create new laws and institutions to deal with issues like electronic commerce, obscenity on the Internet, and protection of privacy in a fully-networked environment. Because the Information Age is so different from the Industrial Age, even the most mundane old problems often require new and unprecedented kinds of answers.

This book has dealt with the structure of our civil justice system. Others who are concerned about the future of the system are addressing the equally daunting task of looking at changes in the law itself. David Johnson and David Post of the Cyberspace Law Institute, for example, are looking at how to regulate disputes that occur solely in cyberspace, and how rules of jurisdiction will have to change. Their research has led them to conclude that: "Many of the jurisdictional and substantive quandaries raised by border-crossing electronic communications could be resolved by one simple principle: conceiving of Cyberspace as a distinct 'place' for purposes of legal analysis by recognizing a legally significant border between Cyberspace and the 'real world.'"[1]

Another analyst, Philip Howard, has written extensively and often hilariously about the adverse effects of an overabundance of Industrial Age regulation in an emerging Information Age world.[2] In an increasingly mobile environment, activities can fall within the laws and regulations of a multitude of jurisdictions. Sometimes these laws and regulations will conflict with each other. Similarly, in the computer age there is almost no limit to the number of common law precedents and analogies that can be presented to a judge who is seeking the applicable law to apply to a case. As one lawyer puts it: "[L]awyers face an abundance of law disguising a near-complete inability to answer a legal question. In an era of too much law, there is always something for everyone."[3] Here too, the CORE Court system might help. Each Court, through its specific procedures, could address the question of how rationally to limit precedents and analogies. This is just one more aspect of a basic Information Age problem everyone faces: how to keep from drowning in data.

I am, admittedly, future oriented. I live in a world in which I communicate daily, via the Internet, with people all around the globe. I watch with fascination as millions of people come "online" every few months. I observe, up close, how businesses, schools, and even governments are using the Internet to change their operations fundamentally. Schools now enroll students whom they will never see in person, only through the Internet. Businesses, even in this early stage of electronic commerce, already are buying and selling goods over the Internet . . . not to mention the growth of Internet advertising. Governments are seriously considering how citizens can submit required forms and registrations and even pay their taxes over the Internet. I have attended on-line meetings and conventions where participants hear speeches and carry on interactive discussions without ever being in the same physical location.

If my own experiences are not yet commonplace, neither are they unique. Millions of people move or are drawn into this new world every year. The Web grows ever larger, more complex. Indeed, some economists are suggesting that the Internet and computers will drive rapid economic growth in the same way that different industries did as they came "on-line" during the Industrial Age: automobiles in the 1920s, aviation during and after World War II, consumer electronics in the 70s and 80s. Just as these industries created jobs by the millions, the Information Age has already created millions of new positions for software programmers, chip makers, virtual realists, computer consultants, and others. Peter Drucker calls them "technologists" and "knowledge workers," and estimates that such workers will comprise at least a third of the American work force by the end of the century, "as large a proportion as manufacturing workers ever made up [during the Industrial Age] except in wartime."[4]

We joke in my industry about "Internet Time," which is very fast. The Internet creates enormous efficiencies in communication, and these efficiencies in turn allow for greater efficiencies in work. Increasingly, the Information Age is evolving at the speed of Internet time, which means that the social and economic changes of the Information Revolution will probably occur more quickly than might be expected, based upon historical precedent. In law, we are already in a state of chronic crisis. The crisis may "go critical" very shortly. As with all critical moments, they come about through a confluence of factors.

- If and as ever more litigants move their disputes to the ADR system, the common law will cease to evolve in an adequate way.

- If and as ever more citizens become disgusted with the failure of the courts to deliver just (or at least tolerable) results, or fed up with the high cost of litigation, or with the amount of time involved, then they may resort to more direct and aggressive methods of resolution . . . and retribution.

- If and as ever more judges and lawyers become disheartened by the unhealthy state of the profession and the legal system, then we will lose the very people most qualified to restore its health.

Our quest for justice may be sacred. Our civil justice system, in its present form, is not. It can and must be changed. It is a system instituted by the American Founders and modified by their descendants to handle day-to-day problems. As these problems change, the problem-solving system must also change if it is to continue to fulfill its function. Given the immensity of the changes coming upon us, tepid and half-hearted tinkering will not be enough, and may indeed lead to a misplaced and potentially disastrous sense of false security. We must stop pretending, denying, and protesting when it comes to legal reform. We must do what the Founders and their descendants did. We must start thinking and acting. As their heirs, we inherit both their institutions and their tradition of meaningful and effective reform.

However, we must also recognize that this effort is not the monopoly of legislators, judges, and lawyers. Every citizen is affected by the civil justice system. Every voter has a role. So does every juror. So does every litigant. This is everybody's problem.

In order to refresh the civil justice system, there are immediate tasks and there are long-term tasks. The immediate tasks involve correcting some of the more egregious dysfunctions and abuses. This must be primarily the work of judges, lawyers, and clients. For those attorneys – a small minority – who callously exploit and exacerbate the system's failures, an honest self-appraisal may be too much to expect. Some of these lawyers no doubt believe that this is how the world is supposed to work. As long as you don't explicitly and egregiously break the rules (or get caught breaking the rules), the clever are entitled to take advantage of the less clever. This type of lawyer won't get the message until it is in his or her personal interest to do so. But for the many lawyers who are unsettled by what they see and experience, yet who have no idea what to do about it, there are plenty of opportunities available.

A final plea and exhortation:

Become an activist regarding the problems you see and experience personally. Think creatively about what the lawyer's problem-solving role needs to be in an Information Age society. Help bring your vision to reality. Senior attorneys: mentor your juniors. And if you are a law school professor, you're uniquely positioned to undertake the reorientation of the profession, away from problem-creating and toward problem-solving.

Clients, too, can make a big difference. This point can be made through a simple (and true) story. One of my friends, on vacation, rented a bike for a short ride around the grounds of a hotel. While on her ride, she took such a bad fall that the bike broke in half. Three weeks later, my friend visited a masseuse, who asked about some muscle stiffness. When told about the accident, the masseuse immediately advised my friend to sue, noting that she would document the muscle stiffness for the lawsuit, as she had for numerous other customers.

So why was this so bad? Because the masseuse had never asked who or what had caused the accident. In fact, the bike and the hotel grounds had both been in fine condition; my friend's fall had simply been an accident. How many people would have done as the masseuse suggested, suing the hotel because of its perceived "deep pockets?" It's a vicious circle – or, to shift metaphors a bit, a vicious downward spiral. The more we see the system abused, the more accepting we become of our own participation in the abuses. Clients can help break that spiral.

The long-term tasks are harder and, given the accelerating rate of change in this society, must be started immediately. These tasks involve restructuring the system, both to make it responsive to the needs of the Information Age and to put Information Age technology to work within the legal system itself. The system must not be undone by the quantity and specificity of 21st century information, flowing through non-geographic interfaces at "Internet Time."

In the Information Age, the ancient principle still holds. Litigants have the right to a fair hearing before decision-makers who possess the relevant information and can understand it. CORE Courts can serve this principle far better than the present system, or the present system only partially reformed.

But the CORE Court system – or any improved system – will not spring into being on its own. The bar associations, the law schools, the courts, and the legislatures need to start considering the enormous task, not just of dealing with issues in cyberspace, but moving justice itself into cyberspace.

So far, there have been relatively few efforts in that direction. However, those underway show promise. I mention several examples.

- *The Virtual Magistrate Project.* This is essentially an ADR program, designed for cyberspace. An experiment undertaken by the National Center for Automated Information Research (NCAIR), the Cyberspace Law Institute, the Villanova Center for Information Law and Policy, and the American Arbitration Association (AAA), "Virtual Magistrate" attempts to solve cyberspace disputes in cyberspace. As an example: Somebody posts an Internet item that may be libelous. The offended party might take the complaint into the physical court system. Or the potential plaintiff might call "Virtual Magistrate," who would assign a mediator to help resolve the dispute, perhaps in accordance with "Netiquette" – the standards prevailing in that part of the Internet.[5] At the moment, the project applies only to Internet problems. But might it not also be seen as a first attempt to move ADR, and perhaps someday even litigation, into cyberspace? Whether "virtual trials" will ever become the norm is debatable. But might it not be a valuable option for those who desire it as an alternative to costly and extended traditional litigation?

- *Electronic Filing.* Some court systems are moving toward greater use of electronic means to expedite paperwork. In 1996, the Northern District of Ohio became probably the first court in the nation to accept filings via the Internet. Two populous counties, Prince George's County in Maryland and Los Angeles County in California, have introduced electronic filing by modem on an experimental basis. Delaware has established a system called Complex Litigation Automated Docket (CLAD) for exclusive use in large cases. And the Stanford University Law School, in cooperation with the Securities and Exchange

Commission and the judges of the United States District Court for the Northern District of California, has established a special web site to provide on-line information and analyses related to state and federal securities fraud suits. It's called the Securities Fraud Class Action Litigation Clearinghouse.[6]

- *On-Line Motion Project.* This is a particularly exciting experiment planned for certain federal district courts in the Northern District of California. It will permit attorneys to file and respond to various motions without the necessity of physically going to the courthouse. Interactions among attorneys and judges will all take place on the Internet. The savings in time and expense could be enormous.

- *Project Argonaut.* Another ambitious on-line project involves nothing less than getting the law, in its entirety, onto the Internet. A new initiative, Project Argonaut, is attempting to determine the feasibility of bringing all U.S. law into a common data base. This effort was announced in 1996 by an organization called Lex Mundi, an association of 125 law firms, with financial backing from various providers of technology and legal services. The goal here is to unify all the legal data bases that are now coming into existence. If completed, the implications for litigation would be substantial.

These efforts matter, and not just because of their attempts to bring new technologies into the system. They are also all cooperative ventures, uniting attorneys, courts, law schools, and technology and service providers. They are paradigms of how to operate in the Information Age, where complexity is the norm and cooperation essential, no matter what the outcome of individual projects.

But for these kinds of changes to occur sooner rather than later, i.e., before crisis turns to catastrophe, it will be necessary for the present generation of leaders, in the bar, the courts, the legislatures, and the law schools to get involved. This means that many of them will have to master their own understandable fears: of new technologies; of threats to self-interest; of reluctance to change an inherently conservative institution such as the law; of reticence in the face of inevitable opposition from colleagues; of the very enormity of the task. After all, as Thomas Jefferson wrote in the Declaration of Independence, forms of government ought not to be changed for "light and transient reasons." But Jefferson also wrote that "any form of government" can become destructive of the ends for which it was established. In that case, it is the right and duty of the people to "alter or abolish it."

Nobody wishes to abolish the civil justice system. But altered it must be, for the sake of the values that the system has always been expected to uphold and advance. The Constitution of the United States specifies that the judicial power of the country will reside in one Supreme Court and in such inferior courts as the Congress may, *from time to time*, create. The Constitution does not specify how such courts shall be organized or operate. That's up to the Congress. And, in a larger, sense, it's up to us.

Today, the American civil justice system exists somewhere between dysfunction and oppression. It's time to call it back and, once again, to be worthy of the Founders' trust, and the traditions and ideals that we have inherited.

1 Quoted in Russell Blinch, "Time to Send in the Internet Mounties," *Canadian Financial Reporter,* November 29, 1996. The full paper, David Johnson and David Post, "Law and Borders – The Rise of Law in Cyberspace," is available from the Cyberspace Law Institute at www.cli.org.

2 See, for example, Philip Howard, *The Death of Common Sense: How Law Is Suffocating America* (New York: Random House, 1995).

3 Anonymous, "A Litigator's Lament," *American Lawyer,* December 1993, at p. 80.

4 See Peter Drucker, "The Age of Social Transformation," *Atlantic Monthly,* November 1994, at p. 53.

5 See "The Virtual Magistrates, " *The American Lawyer's Corporate Counsel Magazine,* June 1996, at p. 56. See also Henry H. Perritt, Jr., "Proceedings of a Conference on Electronic Dispute Resolution," sponsored by NCAIR, May 22, 1996.

6 See Henry J. Reske, "An Internet Road to Court," *ABA Journal,* November 1996, at p. 34; Arleen Jacobius, "Two More Courts Add Electronic Filing," *ABA Journal,* September 1995, at p. 20; Stanford Law School Press Release, 6 December 1996, "Shareholders Gain First Time Access to Securities Fraud Suits."